FUNCTIONAL SILENCE

DE-MYSTIFYING AWAKENING FOR THE SPIRITUALLY EXHAUSTED

Gabor Harsanyi
With co-author Nurit Oren

Published by Gabor Harsanyi

Budapest, Hungary

Book cover and internal design by Jane Green of Everlasting Magic Design.

design@everlastingmagic.com

Cover painting and drawings by Kornelia Sen

Photos of authors by Eva Harsanyi

ISBN – 978-963-12-8607-6

IN PRAISE OF FUNCTIONAL SILENCE

"This book is a goldmine of liberating hints and is a *'must read'* for anyone who is searching for guidance in this jungle of misleading information. I am simply delighted. I find the expressions and metaphors beautiful, enlightening and simply helpful to anyone who wishes to escape from the slavery that we have been conditioned to believe to be freedom. I am overwhelmed by the beauty, clarity and thoroughness of this work. In short, I have not read anything in this book that I could not sign. In Love, Samarpan"

Samarpan, satsang teacher, public speaker

"I have just finished reading the book *'Functional Silence - De-Mystifying Awakening for the Spiritually Exhausted'* and I loved it for its simplicity, wisdom of direction and very sound pointers. I have known Gabor Harsanyi for many years and when I left Toronto in 1984 he was still a seeker. When I watched him, years later, on U.K. Conscious TV I saw a man who found himself. Gabor wrote in this book *'As the creator, would you make the road difficult for your children to return Home?'* In like manner Gabor's book is designed to open the eyes to the possibility of a new way of seeing the simplicity and obviousness of the reality of Life. I highly recommend this book to anyone who is serious about waking up to the truth of Being. Thank you Nurit and Gabor for this privilege. Love, Burt"

Burt Harding, author, spiritual teacher, founder of Awareness Foundation

"Stunningly effective! It's a 'God-Book' that should be read several times."

Bill Cael, international teacher and healer, founder of Soundbody Int.

DECLARATIONS OF GRATITUDE

First and foremost, I would like to acknowledge and offer my deep gratitude to my ex-wife, **Lupita Hartwig**, who is the angel that made it possible for me to survive the pain of leaving home in search for Truth, in spite of the pain that my leaving has inflicted on her.

My beloved children, **Jason, Marlen and Mariana**, also stood by me and never stopped showing their love even though, my unconventional fatherly behaviour took me away from them, in pursuit of my spiritual fulfillment.

My dear brother **Tom**, you have always been a constant pillar of support in my life! I will never forget your kindness.

Next, I wish to acknowledge the great Cosmic Troubadour, **Iby Duba**, who inspired me to delve into the yet-unrevealed and underestimated treasures of the Magyar language, which provided for me an unparalleled platform for explaining the unexplainable.

Another great benefactor, who offered many hours of assistance, unconditional support and much needed friendship during the preliminary phase of my writings, is the wonderful reporter and author, **Illes Sarolta**, to whom many thanks are offered. She was also very instrumental in getting me started by creating my first few videos, including the one called "Functional Silence".

And, of course, the enthusiasm and genuineness of the highly accomplished and brilliant **Dr. Szasz Ilma** is also tremendously appreciated. With all her heart, soul and splendid intellect, she has demonstrated time and again her incomparable commitment to making this work known to sincere seekers.

Many thanks to **Ian McNay** of Conscious.TV and to **Rick Archer** of Buddha at the Gas Pump for granting me wonderful platforms to share my work through their highly proficient interviewing skills. Their efforts to raise spiritual awareness is of utmost importance and very much appreciated.

I also wish to acknowledge my first teacher, **Burt Harding**, for giving me the foundation and the first push in the right direction towards awakening. Thank you so much Burt, for taking the time to read the manuscript of this book and for writing a wonderful heart-felt review.

Beloved **Samarpan**! Your words of acknowledgment for this book far exceed anything I can say. They filled Nurit and I with tears of gratitude and awe. Thank you so much!

Much appreciation from my heart also goes to my dear friend **Stefan Hiene**, for his undying love, support, advice and beautiful words of acknowledgment.

Another friend who has been there for Nurit and I right from the start is **Bill Cael**, who took time out of his busy schedule to read the manuscript several times, considering it to be a "God-book". Thank you for your precious words of appreciation dear Bill!

Many thanks also to the wonderful friends, students and advocates of this work – **Janna Gougeon, Dorina Dumitrescu, György Liptovszky, Pierre Richard, Andras Petz, Attila Hack, Birgitta Süss and Boudewijn Zweerts** – for your inner-recognitions, commitment to awakening and your beautiful testimonials that acknowledge the magic of our sacred connection, and allow others to get a glimpse of this unity.

What an honor to have one of Guthema Roba's beautiful poems as an opening to my book! Thank you so much brother Guthema for this gift of poetry.

The drawings in this book are as a result of the countless hours that our dear friend and remarkable artist, **Kornelia Sen**, devoted to pouring her heart and soul into creating - making sure they fit the words that wished to be expressed in this book. Thank you so much, beloved Kornelia, for your amazing dedication and selfless endeavours of love, and for bringing out the humour, levity and visual aspects of this work.

Many thanks to **Jane Green** of Everlasting Magic Design, for the amazing interior and cover design of the book, and to **Lindy Booth** for her expert editing.

And, last but not least, I wish to express my eternal gratitude to my beloved wife, partner, co-author and best friend, **Nurit Oren**, who has skillfully and successfully managed to transmute my heart and soul into words, and to make the nearly inexpressible accessible to others. She stood by me through thick and thin and supported me with her love and dedication through many difficult moments. Most importantly, she partnered with me in consciousness, and used conscious-presence to navigate with me through life's challenges and successes.

With much love and appreciation,
Gabor Harsanyi - Budapest, Hungary – Apr 13, 2017

TABLE OF CONTENTS

THE LAUNCHING PAD – THE "GOLDEN RATIO GATE" - THE ENTRANCE INTO "HOME"

THE "GOLDEN RATIO GATE" AT THE 4TH PROGRESSION

ATTENTION... IS THE MAGICAL KEY TO THE "GOLDEN RATIO GATE"

4th PROGRESSION – GEOMETRICAL PERSPECTIVE

WARNING! LAUNCHING ERROR! ROCKET WITH TAXI MENTALITY!

SIRENS AT THE GATES

FIRING UP FOR TAKE-OFF! ARE WE THERE YET???

CONTEXTUAL SHIFT AT THE "GOLDEN RATIO GATE"

POEM BY GUTHEMA
- A MODERN-DAY HAFIZ

Put aside other things
for now
and pay attention
to what is continuously
burning,
the eternal within you,
inside this dissolving,
inside this burning,
the universe becomes
transformed and anointed
because you're willing
to see yourself
not as a local person
but as a cosmic being –
and whatever you do
locally elevates everyone
around you.

Infinite love and blessings,
Guthema Roba, Apr 10, 2017

READER'S "IN-GEST"
(by Nurit Oren)

Evolution

"Who am I?"

"Who is the observer?"

After 40 years of asking myself these questions, searching, studying, meditating, chanting, serving and after pondering those made-up mystical questions that weren't mine to begin with, I **FINALLY** asked myself **my own** questions:

"Why the hell am I still searching after all these years?"

"Why am I still doing the same thing, if I am getting the same **'no-result?'**"

"Where is this path taking me **REALLY**?"

"Where is the big prize of **awakening**, I was promised - if I did this, that and the other - which I did?"

Well, wouldn't you know it! My own questions seemed much more fruitful! They led me to find Gabor, my awakening guide, who did not make me spend years of hard work followed by "waiting" and did not judge my former spiritual "naivete" (folly is more like it, but I learned to be kind to myself). On the contrary - he accepted me, in spite of my well-endowed spiritual ego, developed by accumulating empty spiritual accolades. He gave me the gift of a lifetime! My days of being a spiritual sheep were over!

Gabor **INSTANTLY** got me to stop my mind **for the first time...** long enough for my own being to recognize itself, and deep enough to perceive that all my previous spiritual "work" (no wonder it was so hard!) was done with the mind. This realization blew the top off my entire spiritual identity, cleaned up my addiction for "searching" and, most importantly, made me see so clearly, that awakening and spirituality are two completely different things. And by "awakening", I mean true awakening from this 3rd dimension contrast reality.

The topic of this book, which is awakening into the silence of presence, is one that is nearly impossible to explain or put into words, but when many of Gabor's friends and students started asking, "When will your book come out?" he felt compelled to do something about finding the words for a book. Unfortunately (or should I say, "fortunate for me!"), Gabor can't write. He can speak exceptionally well from presence and has amazing clarity on this subject, that has been pouring from his being pretty much every waking hour of every day for the past several years. However, asking him to put his ideas and words on paper is like asking an elephant to scratch a porcupine's back.

"So how did this book come about?" you ask! Well, it has been a dance of presence - a co-creation of mind and no-mind, of silence and sound, and, most importantly, the space where these opposite words meet and cancel each other out by merging with the original ONE.

Ok, I get that I may have lost you with this last sentence, so I will put it in a more comprehensive and descriptive manner. For a long time, Gabor and I have been sitting together for our early morning coffee conversations and at our favourite coffee shops at all hours of the day. In these magical meetings, he would start talking from presence. When I was able to be present enough to meet him where he was speaking *from*, I would usually "get" what he was saying on very deep level. I would then immediately turn to my notepad and allow the creative power of that presence to arrange the words in the right formation, occasionally borrowing a file or two from my "author" archives.

So there you have it! This book is Gabor's gift of presence. The entire context and content of it came from his BEING, and I am so grateful for having had the good fortune of being able to participate in this creative waltz. Not only has it been an extraordinary writing experience for me, but the book itself has been living me - transforming me and deepening me into presence from day one of its inception. It is my hope and wish for everyone reading this book, to engage it with a sense of presence and stillness - as I had to do in order to write it - and may it have the same effect on you that it still has on me.

IN-tent

This book is for those who, knowingly or unknowingly, aspire to awaken. If you have been mistakenly, or inadvertently, pursuing dead-end spirituality and are open to see that a dimensionless dimension beyond this dualistic reality exists and that it is in fact your birthright, then this book is for you. If you are still addicted to spiritual seeking and are not ready to throw in that wet and soggy towel, this book may not be your cup of tea...*for now*.

This book is not intended to fill your heads with new spiritual concepts, but rather to shed light on the many confusing misconceptions about awakening that are rampant in the ever-growing "spiritual" arena. It is our attempt to de-mystify awakening, to take it off its imaginary pedestal and to take the readers as far as we can with words and metaphors. We even brought in words from an ancient language, since they did not lose the original base of Being.

Our intention with this book is not to raise the bar for "more and more" achievements, but rather to raise the floor, metaphorically speaking, so that the reader will find the new platform from which all else is added with ease and effortlessness.

It's Not Rocket Science!

So, I only ask of you the readers, to do yourselves a favor and read this with as little mental interference as you can. Although the metaphor of a rocket is used throughout the book, you will soon come to see that this is not rocket science. If something is not clear to you, read it again. If it is still not clear, don't worry – many topics are repeated in various ways throughout the book and eventually become not only clearer, but deeper. There is also a list below of recommended videos, and it would be very useful and beneficial to watch them in conjunction with the study of this book.

If one takes the direction that is revealed in this book, it will work. The path that is elucidated here is either easy or impossible. It is extremely easy, if the principles are adopted and practiced. By the same token, it is impossible to succeed on the path to awakening if any portion of the mind is attempting to accomplish this.

Using the metaphor of a gymnast – if awakening were like becoming a gymnast, this book will certainly bring you to the entry of the gym. Nevertheless, the gymnast/reader still has to enter the gym and work out. Hanging out in a library and studying the history of gymnastics will yield no tangible results in the direction of becoming a gymnast.

In the same manner, this book points to and even brings one to the gate beyond which, one's birthright of awakening is granted. However, one still has to become humble, empty and naked enough to enter and follow the practices that sustain the new platform of Being that we were meant to enjoy.

No matter how many great Olympic gold-medalists one knows, there will never be any advancement in one's attainment of his/her goal of becoming a gymnast if one has not entered the gym with his/her own body, and actually does the exercises. No matter how many books, visualization techniques or great masters one is familiar with, nothing will happen unless and until one enters the gate of awakening with his/her own body, heart and soul.

As you will find out from reading this book, awakening is on a *feeling* level. It is not a mental process, so you would be wise to read it with emphasis on feeling rather than as a new mental concept to adopt. If you are perturbed by any spelling mistakes or a misplaced comma, know that your mind has taken over. Our focus here is not on literary accuracy, but rather on our interest and intent that you "get" the book's message on a feeling level. At times, we use commas just to get the reader to pause.

There are also many questions from students, the answers to which will help to bring about further clarity. You might notice that similar questions which arise will not always have identical answers. This is because each answer is offered to a different person and, most importantly, at a different moment. Since no moment is the same as another, no answer is the same as another, even when questions seem to spring from a similar source of confusion.

There are certain things, like the nitty-gritty of the "how to", that can only be transmitted in person or in a seminar setting with Gabor, as they are mostly custom made to each individual. Putting them in words would only keep you "thinking" about them, rather than BEING. I have seen and met many of Gabor's students from around the globe, and it has truly been a marvel to witness the quick and effortless awakening of those who are able to imbibe the skill of "effortlessness" that Gabor imparts.

Gabor's students don't sit around him basking in his "Look how I can BE!" state. He does not "sell" himself to his students, but rather "shows" his students a way to find their own authentic Being, with a "Look at how *you* can BE!" approach... making them free and independent. He continuously comes up with new concepts to destroy old false spiritual concepts and then he immediately discards his new made-up ones, so that the freedom from all mental concepts can reign supreme. My prayer for you dear readers, is that you receive this gift of freedom as well.

Nurit Oren, author of "The Blind Leading the Blonde on the Road to Freedom: Confessions of a Recovering Spiritual Junkie"

Recommended Videos:

- Gabor Harsanyi on Conscious.TV
  https://www.youtube.com/watch?v=RsVBapY8jC8&t=53s

- Functional Silence
  https://www.youtube.com/watch?v=2g4luu31p0I&t=549s

- Gabor Harsanyi - Buddha at the Gas Pump
  https://www.youtube.com/watch?v=JRb_5Qzt0sU&t=867s

- An Experience of Going Within
  https://www.youtube.com/watch?v=JJfWBrCQRko

- How to Be Present in Challenging Situations
  https://www.youtube.com/watch?v=x6mnRhHUFlE

FUNCTIONAL SILENCE

DE-MYSTIFYING AWAKENING FOR THE SPIRITUALLY EXHAUSTED

Gabor Harsanyi
With co-author Nurit Oren

<u>GROUND ZERO</u>

THE ROCKET THAT THINKS IT'S A TAXI

WAITING FOR OUR TURN...OR CLAIMING OUR BIRTHRIGHT?

Are We Operating on All Cylinders?

Last Sunday, one of my students, a lovely elderly lady, called me and frantically said, "Your videos! I can't find your videos! They were all in my computer and now they're gone."

"What do you mean?" I asked.

"I just moved to Budapest to be closer to your satsangs. I have the same computer that I used before to see your videos, but now I can't find them."

"Is your internet connection activated?" I inquired.

"Oh!" she paused. "I guess I need to call my internet provider and get connected."

"That would be a good idea." I replied. "All the programs are still "inside", but they need to be re-activated by connecting to the world-wide web."

The cosmic intelligence web - the creator - created human beings with many God-like abilities. These are not "gifts", but rather our birth right... our in-heritance... since all the ingredients of these abilities are factory-built in, just as various operating systems are built into our computers. However, without being activated by connecting to the source,

> Our current reality is a contrast-reality, since its objects and concepts are recognized through opposites – hate/love, dark/light, etc.
>
> The reality we awaken to is a unifying reality as it unites us with all existence.

Disclaimer:

This is not a legal disclaimer. It is rather a "facts" disclaimer. All the facts, used in this book, are believed to be correct. However, we cannot get to awakening by using "proven" facts.

Therefore, the explanations that are used in this book are based on how helpful or useful they are in reaching our goal. Once awakening has taken place, we can make up whatever facts we want.

these wonderful facilities won't work. We have the built-in ability to soar like rockets beyond our imagination, but we seem to be stuck in our "taxi-identity".

Among the abilities that we have, there are two that are most noteworthy. One is significant since it is very much "activated" and it helps us navigate the world we live in, which I usually refer to as the world of contrast-reality, since its objects and concepts are recognized and referenced through their opposites - hate is hate, since it is not love; dark is dark since it is not light, etc. This ability is what allows us to interact with our world by making distinctions. We are able to see, define, compare, analyse, draw conclusions, create mental templates etc. in this world of contrasts.

The other important ability is within us and is active at birth, but soon becomes dormant and de-activated, as we grow into our overly developed intellectual pursuits. This is the faculty that, once re-activated, can allow us to interface with the world on a more universal scale, where the world is no longer perceived as a separate and scary entity of differences and conflicts, but rather **felt** as a sense of unity with all existence. This will be explained in more detail in the upcoming chapters of this book.

When only the "contrast reality interface sensor" is activated.

When both the "contrast reality interface sensor" & the "instrument of unification" are activated.

If both the abilities mentioned above were activated, humans would be perfectly equipped to thrive and soar in this world as well-functioning, integrated and synergistic beings, and so-called magic and miracles would be realized as natural everyday occurrences. However, this is not the case. Currently only the first one – the contrast-reality interface sensor – is activated. The other one – the instrument of the unification of all existence – although it is "within" us, has been atrophied and therefore it must be re-activated if humanity is to get back to its origin.

This is a big problem, since 99% of our world is in the realm of "non-sense", the realm that can only be accessed through the yet un-awakened ability. Thus, we have been greatly handicapped and have been forced to interact, make decisions and carve out a life for ourselves with limited and insufficient faculties. We are shut off from interfacing with the rest of existence in a full manner as we were originally meant to, as sons and daughters of our creator.

No wonder we created a world as it is today. Problems cannot be resolved by consistently limiting our reality, as is the norm in the contrast-reality. We need to wake up from this dormant state. This is what awakening is all about. It is not awakening from one contrast-reality to another. Realizing that humanity has been controlled and manipulated and standing tall in our new identity and a slightly different contrast-reality is not true awakening. Awakening is simply the self-activation of the lost ability to interface with all existence in a unifying manner.

> **Awakening is the Self-Activating ability inherent within us...**
> **as Being recognizes itself!**

Eagle Identity Crisis

This is what this work is about. Without this activation, we are forever stuck in the cycle of crisis, critical mass and harmful resolutions. In this restrictive and self-destructive way of living, we go deeper into the comatose of delusion and we start acting like an eagle with crippled wings. Once a powerful eagle loses its wings, its stature and quality of life are greatly diminished. Just like a chicken, it now feeds on crumbs off the ground and drags its weight around on foot... along with its false identity.

The eagle, once a majestic soaring beast, is now reduced to a pathetic creature that is forced to mingle with chickens, eat crumbs off the ground, and navigate on foot, without ever being able to soar to the heights that are its birthright.

Awakening is our birthright! And yet it has been kept hidden from us by grandiose spiritual promises of a ***future*** reward that we must earn. It has been covered up with layers and layers of mystical bullshit and secrets, generated by huge spiritual egos disguised as humble servants of God.

As the Creator, Would You Make the Road Difficult for Your Children to Return HOME?

This book is in no way a substitute for the initiation and practice of re-proportioning the attention and the integration process that follows, which are all taught and imbibed in my seminars and private sessions.

This book answers the prevalent question, "Why should I bother doing something so simple, when it doesn't excite my mind? There is so much mysticism, so many exciting motivational types of teachings and organizations (even though they are totally missing the point) and so many varieties and spiritual carrots out there, consistently dangling in front of my nose. They all allow me to hang on to my old ways of thinking, while pretending to offer sensational transformation."

> The difficulties on the path are man-made! This book is about to expose how these came about, for the sole purpose of pointing out how easy it really is to awaken, once the self-made obstacles are removed.

When the people I work with are willing to put the techniques for awakening into practice in their daily lives, these exercises, when repeated often, never fail to bring about the required transformation and exceptional results.

This is not stated for me to take credit for the success rate of my students. On the contrary! It is rather a testament to the Creator's intended intensity to break down the thin veil that the mind seems to hold so precious. Why on earth (no pun intended) would the Creator make it hard for his millions of children to return HOME? After all, if you were the Creator, would you make the road difficult for *your* children to return HOME?

The Sinking Boat

It is obvious that something is very wrong in the world we live in. You don't need to be highly educated, extremely smart, a mystic, a psychic or even intuitive to recognize this. I bet if you turned on CNN right now (or any other biased, misleading or manipulative news channel), you would be watching some disaster or other – mostly man made. And yet, it is also correct that everything, including you, is the way it should be.

We live in this world as if it were an imaginary sinking boat that is filled with holes. The human experience has been one of struggle and strife with conflicts and wars. We assume that we have to keep searching for ways to plug the holes in this ship to keep it afloat. In spite of the brilliant scientists and philosophers and some of the great religions, we have established a value system that corresponds with the plugging of these holes. Anything that can plug the holes is of value to us, and money is on the top of that list of values.

> As we move on, we will be transcending our own expressions. Any other way of teaching this would only set mental traps.

In a universe that is an open and ever-expanding system, we have created a closed, contrasted and contracted life-style. This kind of life-style has become a cancer to this planet. It seems that, if the planet has been entrusted to us, we are not very good caretakers of it.

Awakening is simple, and I wish to share with you an elevated platform of simplicity. All that is needed is to discard the imaginary holes that we feel so compelled to plug. We have become so accustomed and familiar with complexities that our minds may want nothing to do with simplicity and will attempt to reject it every step of the way. Hence this book – to get the mind to be willing to give this a shot.

The explanations here are gradient in nature. In other words, the steps to take are discussed and shown, and words are used, even though the topic spoken of is one which is not in language. Thus, in each new "level", the words and the steps that preceded may be discarded as they may no longer be relevant in the next phase.

I realize that this, of course, is contrary to the accumulation of explanations and concepts, as is the norm in regular learning. Nonetheless, I reserve the right to abandon and leave behind any expressions, terminologies and even techniques that may have been stated in earlier steps.

Any other way of teaching this would only set mental traps. The intention here is to train the mind to function in a different environment, while being in this one. If we could fly, most things we did in walking wouldn't be applicable. The teaching is meant for people to function from the space of presence. Presence comes about as a result of instant interruption of linear time. It is independent of any sequential event or accumulated information. It can only be experienced "now" by going within.

Chewed Up Bones

There is not much out there in the way of encouragement to go within, with the exception of repetitive words, that have been so over-used and, thus, have lost their meaning and lustre. I call these "chewed up bones". However, there is plenty of opposition – often violent in nature – and an abundance of obvious and subtle reasons that the mind will use to con you into looking anywhere but "INSIDE", and anytime but "NOW".

So, dear readers, this book is designed to open your eyes to the possibility of a new value system that will take your life to an elevated platform, where the concepts of "good or bad", "happy or sad", "functional or dysfunctional" etc., become irrelevant and no longer have a hold on you. This is true FREEDOM! And may you all own it and enjoy its magic!

**Let us boldly claim our birthright!
Let us give up the slave attitude of
"waiting patiently for our turn"!**

THE SWORD OF TRANSFORMATION

The Universe is Knocking on Our Doors

Life is happening, bringing with it a huge sword of transformation. You may not be interested in transformation, but it is interested in you. The entire galaxy is pushing for awakening, and we are not exempt. In the face of this thrust we have two choices:

a. To continue to have a consistently difficult life with its incessant swings, that are based on the fear of impermanency.

b. To suffer through some "birth-pains" of transformation, which will eventually be less and less painful. These "birth-pains" will not be in vain, since the well-being and joy that will be delivered, will be permanent.

Allow me to repeat this very important point, so that there are no misunderstandings: I am not saying that there will be no more challenges after awakening. However, these are simply labour pains, which eventually end. The other type of suffering – the duality-created "hell-suffering" – is ongoing and lasts forever. It also seems to continuously be getting worse, since the universe tends to create difficulties and calamities in its attempt to knock on our doors.

Our duality-created "hell-suffering" seems to continuously be getting worse, since this is the way that the universe is knocking on our doors.

We may not be interested in awakening, but awakening is interested in us!

The universe is knocking on our door...and it **WILL** be opened...like it or not!

This is its wake-up call to us! The game is changing. We are meant to be elevated to a new reality, and trying to hold on to the old existing one only results in more pain. Bottom line, the universe is pregnant and it is about to give birth to a new existence. Resisting it would be like a larva refusing to get out of its cocoon and become a butterfly, or like a pregnant woman who refuses to give birth to her child. Good luck!

At present we are chasing durability in a world that is not lasting. Nothing else but allowing the full transformation to occur, is required of us or expected of us. This is what we are being pushed into. The transformational hurricane may be scary, but turning our backs on it is like attempting to protect ourselves from a hurricane in full swing by using an umbrella.

The transformational twister may be scary, but turning our backs on it is even scarier. Attempting to protect ourselves from it, is like trying to open an umbrella when a hurricane is in full swing.

We behave as if life is an obstacle course and then we die. We are consistently striving for happiness in an environment that is permeated with institutionally induced fear and manipulation. We can't fight against evil. We must ascend to a higher platform.

I Just Want to Be Happy... Is That So Wrong?

Question by Linda Jones: *I am a life coach and I live in Los Angeles. I speak with many people about the meaning of life in general and about their life purpose specifically. 99% of them say that all they want is to be happy and secure. Is that not natural for a human being to want that?*

Gabor: *Are you asking them how they are going about achieving that happiness and security they so cherish?*

Linda: *Oh, Of course. That is a big part of our conversation, and I would say at least 90% of them, if not more, say that they have a prominent position with long working hours, or else they have two jobs; they attempt to pay off their mortgage, to put funds aside for the children's education and for their retirement.*

Gabor: *That is perfectly understandable and, of course, it is natural for humans to want to be happy and secure. It is a huge part of our conditioning. Our goals have become "chain loosening" goals, because that is all we are aware of, since that is what our parents were aware of and passed it on to us.*

At present, all we have is a slavery mentality, and this presents the options of better jobs, savings programs with higher interest rates, a more comprehensive health insurance plan, an improved education system, etc. etc. etc. Those are the choices we have under our current circumstances.

In previous centuries, the slaves, the peasants and the lowest casts were only aware of a limited number of options that were available to them. Among them were: obtaining better food, clothing and shelter and avoiding getting beaten, raped or shot by their owners or masters. Quite frankly, not much has changed. What we have now is controlled slavery that is self-induced by our own minds. It is institutionally supported and is also reinforced by society at large.

Something within us wants to be free of all this, but if we attempt to step out of the normal behavior patterns, our neighbours, friends, family members, various institutions and, especially our own minds, will quickly do everything in their power to whip us back into the approved, accepted and authorized slave path.

My Insatiable Hunger for Freedom

Linda: How was it for you prior to your awakening? What was your life like? What was it in your experience that drove you?

Gabor: Well, it is said that the Universe goes through a process of involution, in which out of pure consciousness it begins to create, create and create, thus incarnating into what appears as the world of matter and manifestations. This creation is sustained for a while. Consciousness gets to experience itself in various forms and then starts the process of evolution. This is where the dissolving of creation and the pulling back into itself occurs on a Universal scale, so that it can return to its pure essence.

This is very much the way my life has unfolded. I started out as an innocent, simple and sensitive child, whose primary companions were creatures of nature such as bugs, flowers, trees, etc. However, I was also engulfed and surrounded by emotional upheaval, violence and heartless behavior, which were the norm during the years that Eastern Europe *was attempting to recover from the Second World War, while struggling with its new tyrant, the communist regime. As a result, I soon began to accumulate much fear, anguish and anxiety. The world I lived in was losing its lustre and looking more and more like a bloody mad house!*

Before too long I developed an insatiable hunger for freedom and this feeling accompanied me in various forms throughout my life. It became my primary drive, my leading motivation and sole desire, pushing me and guiding me through ambitious endeavours as well as risky escapes – all to break away from the chains of fear that society had placed upon me. This was my view of life, and it was what propelled me to excel in my studies in high school. I had to do exceptionally well so that I could beat society at its own games.

So, although I was born like an angel, as most children are, I quickly adopted the notion that freedom was "out there", and that I had to fight for it. When I was three or four years old, I dug a hole under the fence in my parents' back yard, just as a dog would. Out I went, hitch-hiking on a horse and buggy. This was my first escape! Ah! My parents, of course, were worried sick about my disappearance, but for me it was the pleasure of freedom... that lasted one full day! I could never stand any kind of bondage.

> **Although I was born like an angel, as most children are, I quickly adopted the notion that freedom was "out there" and that I had to fight for it.**

Fleeing from Communist Hungary to the Trap of Success

Linda: *It must have been rough living in Hungary in those years of oppression.*

Gabor: *Yes... especially for my parents, who did everything they could to shield and protect me and to provide the basic life necessities for me. It was very tough emotionally, since I could feel the oppression and the fear that plagued the country like an epidemic. So, this led to my second escape, when I fled from communist Hungary in 1967. It was a* big deal at the time. I waited until I was 18 years old, so that the full legal responsibility would fall on me and not on my father.

After reaching Yugoslavia, I had to cross another border to Italy. This crossing was very dangerous. However, I felt as though the universe was yanking me out of my previous reality and into a new world. My first three days in Italy were filled with fear and anxiety. I had no idea what to do. I had no money and could not speak a word of Italian. I slept in a telephone booth and prostitutes brought me sandwiches. I was very moved by their kindness. Someone pointed the police station out to me, suggesting I go there and claim refugee status.

So before reaching my final destination, Canada, I spent six months in a refugee camp in Italy, a place of uncertainly and volatility. Nonetheless, I was grateful to be here, since I discovered the feeling of hope. This was a new experience for me. I learned that, no matter how tough my life had become, if I had hope, I could tolerate anything.

In retrospect, I was always driven by a determination and an intense need for inner freedom, although at this point it was still an outer freedom that I was going for. My sense was that if I got away from communism and went "elsewhere", I could be free to make money and release myself from the clutches of other people and the fear they had instilled in me.

> **I was always driven by an intense desire for freedom. However, in those early days, it was still an outer freedom that I was going for.**

I finally arrived in Canada and although I had achieved the outer freedom by escaping from my native country, I was far from knowing true freedom. The need to protect myself and get away from controlling and fear-instilling people and circumstances was still a primary motivator for me. The only difference here was that now I knew the meaning of "hope". I felt that, fueled with this new sense of hope, my intense thirst for freedom could be quenched by my strong drive for success.

Success to me meant having lots of money, a powerful position and *physical strength. My firm belief was that outer protection plus power equalled freedom. So, led by this conviction, I started my own company in real estate, studied martial arts and basically did everything I could to increase my outer strength, wealth and power.*

With this kind of intense ambition, I was able to succeed very quickly. By the time I was 30 years old I was a multi-millionaire. I had more money than anyone I knew, better lawyers, a stronger physique and more accomplishments in martial arts, including a black belt in Hap-ki-do, than most people my age... Bottom line, I was more powerful than the next dude. So, "Don't anyone mess with me!" was my attitude and way of life at that time. Here I was again, now believing that I was gaining freedom out there by engaging in outer achievements in order to obtain it.

I was at the top of my game, with a beautiful and devoted wife, three lovely children and my own successful corporation that was making me rich by the moment. At this point, although I dabbled slightly in spirituality, I was not too serious about it. I had everything I thought I wanted. I was now 40 years old, living the ideal "life" ... so why was I so miserable? Why did I have to drink myself to sleep every night? Something was still very much "off". It became very clear to me that money, power and strength were not giving me the happiness or freedom I was craving, but rather they were just different kinds of chains.

> **It became very clear to me that money, power and strength were not giving me the happiness or freedom I was craving, but rather, they were just different kinds of chains.**

The Relentless Pull of the Universe is Undeniable

Linda: *So, what I am hearing is that what you thought would make you free and happy was actually doing the opposite. So how did you continue to pursue your freedom from this point?*

Gabor: *It was the end of the 80's and many changes took place. The real estate market crashed and with it went all my money. I lost just about everything! Coincidently, I also happened to see a video of Ramtha from The Ramtha School of Enlightenment, which left me feeling that I* absolutely had to learn Ramtha's teachings. Suddenly, and with all these events happening simultaneously, there was a burning desire within me to leave home and go to The Ramtha School of Enlightenment.

Once again, the relentless pull towards freedom took over, as the universe was yanking me out of my current reality. It was pulling me away from my comfort zone and the conventional life style I had. Everything that I held dear collapsed and was taken away from me. The hardest thing I ever had to do was leaving my family, but it had to be done. It was time for a complete change in the direction of my life and there was no stopping it.

> Once again, the relentless pull towards freedom took over, as the universe was yanking me out of my current reality. My comfort zone and the conventional life style I had were snatched away, and everything that I held dear collapsed.

I moved to the west coast of the USA and lived in a forest, while attending Ramtha's school. This was my way of saying "no" to civilization and to all the outer paraphernalia that I have accumulated in an attempt to find happiness and outer freedom. I was now shifting my focus from outer motivation and outer success, as a means to solve my problems, to spirituality. I began to approach spirituality with the same intensity and commitment that I previously had for material success.

My life became driven by an intense spiritual pursuit. I was attending all the classes of Ramtha's school and learning all his techniques, practices, rituals and modes of embodying the teachings – all promising that I would get something at the end. I was having all kinds of mystical experiences, including kundalini awakenings, visions and intense simultaneous "laughing and crying in ecstasy" spells that went on all night. My male ego loved this teaching, because it was non-formal and included extremely intense physical and mental exercises, which really suited my macho and ever-increasing spiritual ego.

At the same time, I also attended every seminar and course within shooting distance of my forest home. I read and studied anything that was even remotely spiritual. I was consistently accumulating more and more amazing spiritual knowledge of all kinds, without ever noticing that I was becoming enslaved by my "search for knowledge" addiction.

Linda: So, what is the solution? What can we do to free ourselves when we don't even realize how enslaved we are?

Gabor: Believe it or not, there is a new road emerging. It has always been there but it has a semblance of being new. It is not only making itself more known to us in all its aspects, but it is also in the process of removing all obstacles and pretty much anything that stands in its way, as it pushes through our veils and takes precedence over all old concepts and limiting slavery paths.

My Existential Shake-Up

Linda: Is that what happened to you?

Gabor: Absolutely! The universe was once again "yanking away" stuff from me, only this time it was determined to wrench out my ego and everything that went with it. It was as if the universe was saying to me, "Wake up or die!" I often refer to this phase of my life as "my final escape" since this time it was not an outer escape like the previous ones – from Hungary or from the material world. This turned out to be an escape within, after which, no further escape is ever needed.

This all took place during a tremendously stressful time in my life. I was living in Mexico and building a condominium complex there, which, in itself, was maddeningly stressful, and I was having all kinds of financial and legal problems to deal with. To top this off, I was experiencing deep suicidal depression, which lasted on and off for approximately 12 years.

> My "final" escape was not an outer escape like the previous ones. This was an escape within, after which, no further escape is ever needed.

It was during this time that I went to Ecuador, where I stayed with an Indian tribe and their shaman for a few months. It was here that I made a most important observation. With all the knowledge, the practices, the techniques, the intellectual embodiment of spiritual concepts etc. that I had acquired during my spiritual phase, I was still not able to just sit and BE, like the Indians did. They had nothing on me in terms of intellectual knowledge, yet they had simplicity and peace, which I so sorely lacked. I had conceptual knowledge of peace, but no experience of peace.

I had to take ayahuasca for several weeks before I could even relax. There was still no great realization or consistent simplicity and stillness as a way of life. Something was still missing and I didn't know that any further development was possible.

> **The Indians had nothing on me in terms of intellectual knowledge, yet they had simplicity and peace, which I so sorely lacked. I had conceptual knowledge of peace, but no experience of peace.**

In retrospect, I still had outer knowledge orientation, but now I had bragging rights, since I was able to be with the Indians and endure the difficulties of surviving in their environment. My male ego was once again getting patched up.

As I returned to Mexico, with all the stress it offered me, the depression was as strong as ever, and there was no inner peace on the horizon. This contributed to my suicidal tendencies. I did everything possible to get rid of the depression, from seeking professional help to using more ayahuasca.

I still had mystical experiences from time to time, including a three-hour experience of swimming blissfully like a dolphin in a pool... However, I was waking up every morning disappointed that I was still alive. I was consistently doubting my need to exist and wanting to disappear from this world altogether. I realized years later, what a gift the depression actually was. Having to question my own existence, which was truly an "existential shake-up", was the closest I could get at that time to my true source of being. It served as a great preparation for what was about to unfold.

How About Looking Inside?

Linda: *My goodness. How did you get out of that one?*

Gabor: *I remember one day, as I was riding my bike to the beach, my mind was filled with thoughts about throwing myself under a bus, followed by thoughts about how this would affect my kids. Somehow, I made it to the beach. As I was standing in front of the water, in my sheer desperation to overcome my depression, the words of Jesus "The kingdom of God is within!" emerged in my being. "What if this is **literally** true?" I wondered. "How about trying to look inside?"*

*I recalled a technique that my Hap-ki-do master taught me when I reached my black-belt. It included feeling the body. Feeling the body turned out to be an essential component, that enabled me to go within. This was a major and instant shift. It was the break-away! The escape this time was from intellectual spirituality. The depression clutches were starting to let go, and although it kept trying to come back and rear its ugly head, I now knew that I had the tool in my hand that was, and still is, the solution to **EVERYTHING**... not only depression.*

Once again I turned in a new direction, but this time it was inner... real inner – not just conceptual and not in the realm of the intellect. This is simple and real inner stillness. My drive now became an inner deepening of this healing and blessed silence.

"Isn't Meditation the Great Liberator?"

Linda: *Isn't that what meditation is supposed to do? Isn't meditation the great liberator that brings about enlightenment?*

Gabor: *Over the years of searching, transforming, resting in my new space of silence and helping others on the way, I have been able to observe how very tricky the mind can be. I have perceived its cunning nature as it attempts to take back its control.*

The mind created the common linear type of meditation so that it could still dominate us, by keeping us pacified and relaxed, while our life is being degraded. Remember, the purpose of this work is awakening. Thus, we evaluate types of meditation and other practices, based on their contribution to awakening.

If linear meditation really worked for awakening, then half the population of California would be enlightened. Since you live in California, I am sure you know that nearly every street corner there has a Starbucks, a meditation and yoga centre and a colon irrigation clinic. Colonics are a great way to clean up and clear out old toxicity from your body. However, we fail to realize that it is equally important to clean up the institutionally supported slavery templates.

Awakening and Being in one's true Home can only be accessed in the present moment. It is instantaneous and beyond the reach of time. The mind on the other hand, has been trained to live in the past or in the future and does not want to let go of its old habitat. It therefore tries to usurp the power of presence by finding ways to insert time into spiritual practices.

Most meditation practices are in time: first of all, they have a beginning and an end; secondly, there is an expectation for something to happen in the near future, such as a vision, a relaxation, an "aha" moment, etc.; thirdly, there is a cumulative expectation, such as achieving a spiritual reward as a result of repetition. In every other pursuit in life, this cumulative approach is great. However, for awakening, we need a completely different approach.

The act of separating oneself from the outer world by closing the eyes, while the mind is still running it its attempts to be spiritual by sitting quietly for a "period of time" does not constitute "going within" and most certainly does not contribute to awakening. It is not the outer world that we want to shut off, but rather the mind.

When you come to my seminars you will learn a different kind of meditation that is not really meditation. It is an "entry" exercise, that facilitates awakening. It has nothing to do with accumulation of spiritual knowledge and practices such as linear meditation. It has to do more with leaping out from the continuity of the mind stream.

Note to readers: More on this later on in this book.

Where Are We Going with This?

In retrospect, all the many practices and techniques I learned and engaged in were like that. They were all time-based with a hope for a future result. I can see now so clearly that practicing "linear" spiritual techniques is a fallacy. It is the mind's current ignorant state that keeps one going around in circles and remaining hooked in time - the mind's only domain and comfort zone. It is all based on the wrong premise, but so many seekers believe in it, so it is an understandable mistake.

What isn't understandable... what seems really stupid to me now, is that no one, including me, ever stopped and asked, "Where are we going with this?" Throughout my years of search, the goal was never clear to me and to others around me, yet this was acceptable.

> **How is it that this loosey-goosey approach to spirituality is acceptable?**

So, What is the Solution?

Linda: *So, what is the solution?*

Gabor: *The solution of course, is the awakening and the activation of our God-given human ability that transcends the duality-based reality and shifts us into a "golden unifying reality". At this point, no matter what we call it, it will sound strange and mysterious. With this newly awakened facility, we will be able to interact with our world by unifying with it. So far, we have only been using the navigation system that we are familiar with, which is the contrast-reality interface.*

In other words, we use our senses to perceive, compare and make distinctions – that's white, that's black, that's good, that's bad, etc. – which, at this point, is very important for survival on this planet. Once our unifying ability is awakened, we will continue to retain our contrast-reality interface, while integrating it with the unifying facility. We will be using both capabilities to function in perfect harmony.

Beyond Facts

Linda: *I can see that it would be very important to have both these capabilities since I believe that even when we are awakened, we still need our discerning abilities to know what the facts are in this confusing world.*

Gabor: *Yes, facts are very important. However, we rarely get them accurately. By the time a fact reaches us, or is conveyed by one to another, it is already contaminated by biased perceptions that interact with and are influenced by, various narrative, habitual mental constructs and templates that are struggling to hold our false identities intact.*

Between books that are translated, the rumour mill and inadequate new age seminars, we are consistently dealing with anything but facts, and thus, we are being manipulated. This makes accurate decision making nearly impossible.

When it comes to awakening, some facts have to be clarified before there is any hope of attempting to do the practices that lead to awakening. At the "point of entry" into awakening however, facts no longer bear the same significance as they did before, and must be completely dropped. This is a paradox that must be accepted – facts are highly important prior to awakening and are completely insignificant during awakening.

> **Facts are highly important prior to awakening... and are completely insignificant during awakening.**

The only reason true facts are so needed at the pre-awakening phase, is that in their absence, the false facts will prevent us from attempting to do any of the practices that would lead to our freedom. The false facts, since they are believed by so many, have tremendous pull and magnetic power. They will pull us back and prevent any attempt at awakening.

There Are No Alternatives in the Realm of Awakening

Linda: *I find it very difficult to know what the facts are, when there are so many alternative paths available these days.*

Gabor: *That's right. Alternatives are in the mind. The purpose of awakening is to step out of the mind, in order to eliminate alternatives. Awakening is not about something to which there are alternatives. In the health field, there are all kinds of alternatives to conventional medicine. In new age and self-improvement modalities, there are all sorts of alternative meditation techniques.*

However, there are NO ALTERNATIVES IN THE REALM OF AWAKENING! We either wake up beyond the mind, or we don't! No amount of mind-modalities work for awakening! The entry to awakening is too narrow for any mind-modality to fit it. It opens by the use of an "angular" key, which is a self-generated "angular leap" out of duality. We either find the right angle, or we don't. (More on this later)

We have many choices when we attend a new age spiritual expo with all the shiny booths that are calling us to: "try this method", "sample my technique", "come to meet my guru... he comes from a long lineage!" etc. Alternatives only exist in the context of the limited mind, where all "self-improvement" modalities thrive, as they offer us an exciting solution to plug the holes in our sinking ship. All these have great value; however, they have no awakening value!

The Spiritual Arena – A Billion Dollar Industry

Question by Shanti Sarah Morgan: *I have been on several spiritual paths for many years and don't feel I am really getting anywhere, and I haven't really seen great results with others. Why are there so few awakened ones, when there are so many seeking?*

Gabor: *In this day and age, it is very easy for misunderstandings to occur, due to the tremendous transformation that has erupted in the hearts of seekers all over the world. There was a time when many people rebelled against religions and became "spiritual". Unfortunately, without true awakening, which is beyond the 3rd dimension, spirituality remains on an intellectual level and merely becomes a new religion with a different name, with different terminology and different activities – yet still on the same level of mind and ego, and seekers who are attempting to be special and have a good life.*

This gave birth to various teachings that sprung up on the scene in order to fulfil a need. Sadly, this situation has also been used to capitalize on the innocence of seekers. Today, many of those spiritual pioneers have become terribly disillusioned, disheartened and disappointed. Some have been fortunate enough to wake up from the "spiritual dream" and various awakened teachers have been very helpful in this process.

"Being Spiritual" as Opposed to Just "BEING"

Shanti: *Yes, I have been very disappointed for quite some time. I don't get why something that is supposed to be simple is so hard to explain.*

Gabor: *One of the most difficult challenges that occurred as this awakening movement began to take on momentum, was finding the way to express or explain the un-explainable, by using the only means available – words – which belong to the realm of duality. It's like trying to fit a square peg in a round hole.*

Another challenge that arose was that many spiritual pioneers have not wanted to awaken, since they have become addicted to the search and to "Being Spiritual" as opposed to just "BEING". In this spiritual dream state, again teachers emerged who have now started to use the few words that the awakened have struggled with, along with some borrowed words from ancient traditions, just to keep the mystery going. The result was that many spiritual dreamers remained comfortably asleep.

The third challenge is that some have awakened "accidentally" and are well meaning in their attempts to help others awaken, but since they don't know how it happened to them, they do not know how to impart this or how to initiate others.

Consequently, we now have a "spiritual arena" which includes:

a. *Many "spiritual dreamers" and their "spiritual gurus/pacifiers" who vacillate between silent retreats and debates about terminology and methodology, throwing around words like "non-duality" or even "awakening" and feeling quite special about their new "spiritual identity", even though they have not had the REAL experience of what they speak about.*

b. *Seekers who intuitively get attracted to awakened teachers who don't know how to teach, but it feels so good.*

c. *Those who have truly awakened into inner silence and who no longer even see themselves as spiritual. Many of them have lost several friends and family members, and perhaps have retained a few covertly hostile acquaintances, who secretly, yet violently, resent the fact that they are no longer bound by the same chains.*

Note to readers: In the context of awakening, losing friends means that we have shed enough of our contrast-reality false identity that these friends can no longer relate to us.

"Self-improvement" type of modalities - with their reputable traditions and ceremonies, originated from a far away past - these imply the promise of awakening, but deliver only: an accumulation of good feelings, behavior modifications, an abundance of knowledge to keep the mind secure, a great future, good fellowship, support, colourful mysticism, and a whole lot of other things... **BUT NOT AWAKENING**.

THE "AHA GATES" - BAGGAGE CONTROL

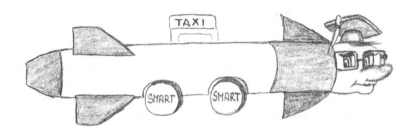

The "Smart Wheels"

The awakening process is very subtle and is beyond the reach of the mind and its conditioning. Jesus referred to it as entering the eye of the needle. I often call it entering the "Golden Ratio Gate", which will soon be elaborated upon. As mentioned before, it is impossible to enter this "Golden Ratio Gate" by using the same methods that we employ when attempting to get ahead in life or ascend to higher stages of understanding on an intellectual level.

To fully get what I mean by this, it is imperative to understand how the mind has been trained to work, and how it strives for higher achievements through what I call the "Aha Gates" or higher and higher steps of understanding and functionality on a mental or intellectual level, or what we can call third dimensional living. (see diagram 1. on the following page.)

Whenever a certain attainment has been achieved or an important realization has been reached, we have our "Aha" moments, in which we feel and think, "Aha! Aha! Now I know!" We then move "up" to the next step/level. (diagram 1 below)

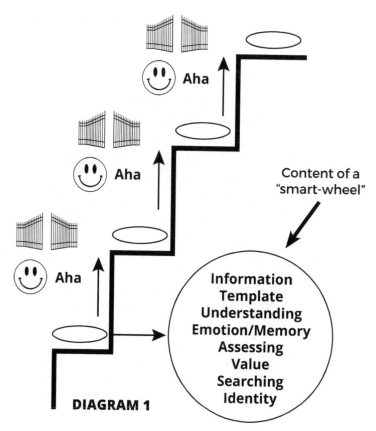

On each horizontal level of diagram 1, we have what I call a "smart wheel". This name is derived from the fact that it contains inter-related mental activities. In each "smart wheel", the following activities are some of the main ones that take place in random order, at the mind's discretion or at times, simultaneously:

- Information gathering and accumulating via the senses

- Pieces of information being compared to one another

- Evaluation of new information and assessment of its relevance to previous information

- Decisions to search for more information

- Templates and narratives are formed

- Understanding of information, templates and narratives - and how they relate to one another

- Storage of all the above

- Nailing down of the above via emotions

And... the two that are the most important to be aware of are:

- **Identity** that is being formed and reformed consistently

- **Values** that are being formulated and/or compared with existing values

> The "Aha" moments feel so good and so new. Some previous concepts and beliefs are left behind, giving us a euphoria that is mistaken for awakening.
> However, this is merely an awakening from one intellectual understanding to another. It too will soon be forgotten.

The significance of these last two lies in the fact that they are the most adverse to awakening. The purpose of Awakening is to discover who we are. The various identities, that are constantly being formed, act as veils that mask this discovery. The values that are being formulated, are all based on fear and survival with the objective of plugging up the holes in our imaginary sinking boat, or loosening up our slavery chains. None of these values is relevant once we awaken, since we realize that there is no sinking boat and there are no chains.

On each of the horizontal steps in diagram 1, the interactive activities in each "smart wheel" operate in a way which is very beneficial in our day to day living. I am speaking about the function that gives us the ability to accumulate information and arrive at more and more advanced conclusions, realizations and understandings. For example, when learning a musical instrument or attempting to build a complex structure like a bridge or a building, it is imperative to gather all the necessary information, to draw conclusions, to use analytical thinking, to put them into templates etc. All these abilities are highly desirable and essential for living on this planet.

Whenever a certain attainment has been achieved or an important realization has been reached, we have our "Aha" moments, in which we feel and think, "Aha! Aha! Now I know!" We then move "up" to the next step/level, as is indicated by the arrows pointing upwards in diagram 1. This is intellectuality at its best! This "Aha" moment of snapping into a "higher level" (enjoy this expression while it lasts, since later on, anything to do with "higher" or "lower" will be invalidated) - we call an "Aha Gate" since it feels like an entry into a new stage.

At times, it feels so good and so new that some previous concepts and beliefs are left behind, giving an euphoria that is mistaken for awakening. However, this is merely an awakening from one intellectual understanding to another... that will soon be forgotten as well.

The "Computerized Smart Wheel"

All the above is fine and good and it explains the modus operandi of our mental/intellectual faculties. It demonstrates their general direction and their penchant to accumulate, to expand and to reach greater heights of knowledge and information that would secure our values and identities. Now let's examine the quality and condition of these inter-relating mental activities.

If a computer program did all the interacting and inter-relating functions that take place on each step of diagram 1, a view from the top would look somewhat like the circles in diagram 2. (see below) All the interactions between the various activities such as information gathering, assessment of the information etc. would look like circles that are neatly placed together and operating in harmony. However, when these are done by a human mind, it is quite different.

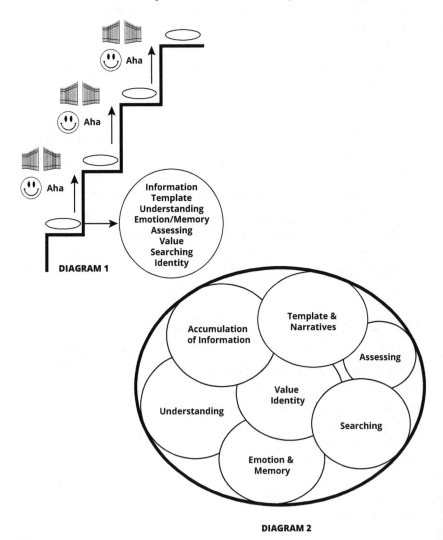

DIAGRAM 1

DIAGRAM 2

The "Human Mind Smart Wheel"

Since the interactive mental activities are done via the human mind, with all its hurts, misconceptions and emotional garbage, the same circles look warped, depending on one's personal value system and the damage done to him or her along the way, as is shown in diagram 3. (see below)

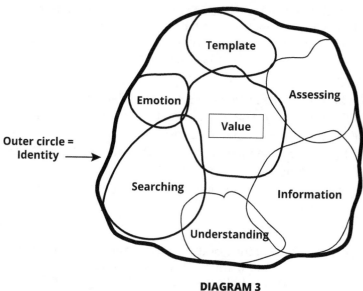

DIAGRAM 3

Taking this into consideration, you can see how moving up the ladder from one "Aha Gate" to another, by utilizing warped and damaged faculties, the world we live in has become bastardized. It is run by insanity.

We have witnessed the human mind's brilliance and genius in the most amazing inventions and creative expressions that have far surpassed the capabilities of a computer. Nonetheless, in its current condition we are also adding madness and often defaulting into destruction, when attempting to solve our problems and protect our identities and value systems.

Resolving Differences in An Open Air Insane Asylum?

We are constantly living under the threat of war, racism is still very much alive, and the divorce rate is at the highest it has ever been. We rarely realize that we are at war with ourselves, as well as with the planet itself. So it should be no surprise that we are living in an open air lunatic asylum.

> **ABSOLUTELY NOTHING BETTER CAN HAPPEN... unless and until we learn how to resolve our differences in a permanent and sustainable way... which is one of the first obvious benefits of awakening.**

We don't have the ability to resolve our differences in a permanent and sustainable way in our present state. It is usually not the question of willingness. Most people would be willing. Some of us realize that in order for things to change, **we** have to change... ***BUT HOW?*** Knowing this as a concept doesn't seem to help. The attempt of this book is to bring about clarity, by identifying the problem and introducing the required skills.

> **With all the brilliance of the human mind and its creative powers, why are there still so many unanswered, fundamental and existential questions in so many minds?**

"How come things are so off?"

"What is the change that is so needed to happen?"

"How come religions haven't solved anything?"

"Why are there so few awakened beings when millions are meditating?"

"Why isn't anyone telling me how to get out of my insanely busy mind?"

Because these questions are all still resounding within the intellectual "Aha Gates" as we have not yet acquired the skill

of "leaping beyond duality", these inquiries do nothing but lead to misguided realizations, conclusions and, at best, temporary solutions:

"Aha! Now I know! I have to improve myself."

"Aha! Let me find a self improvement seminar."

"Aha! I have to find myself."

"Aha! I should go to India?"

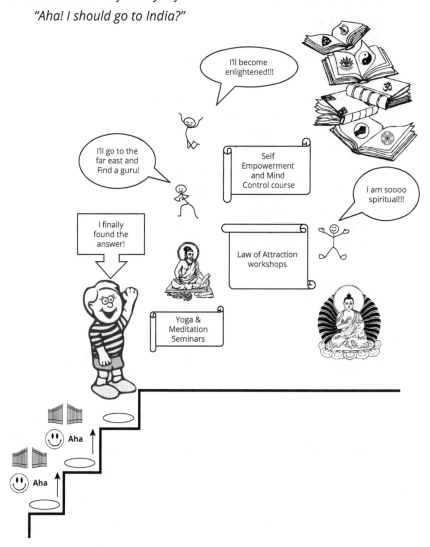

Lineage - An Opportunity for Great Name Dropping!

Question by Kumar Sharma: *I have studied the works of many great Indian teachers of various well known lineages. What is your background in general and what spiritual lineage do you come from?*

Gabor: *I generally dislike speaking about my past. However, since you want to know, I will share a bit with you, in an attempt to make a few essential points.*

As per my general background: I started out with an engineering degree, which later was followed by a business degree from a unique business school in Berkeley, California. Here the emphasis was placed on success and manifestation techniques, leadership, strategic planning and NLP. This experience included studying under Tony Robbins, who was not as famous at that time.

I then became the founder and owner of many successful businesses, which included real estate development, success motivation seminars and more. I facilitated strategic planning sessions for many small and large corporations. I also studied many types of martial arts including Karate, Kung Fu, kick boxing, Aikido and eventually I got my black belt in Hapkido.

Needless to say, I was very much success oriented, and it was highly beneficial to have continuity in my learning. The more techniques and styles I practiced in martial arts, the better I became. In commerce, I experienced the same thing. The more knowledge in different fields of endeavour I acquired, the more successful I became, especially in the strategic planning aspect of the business. So, in this context, accumulation, lineage, and continuity were all very useful.

Having a spiritual lineage provided me with a wonderful opportunity for name dropping and gave me great bragging rights. (laughter...) So, let me now delve into my spiritual lineage:

After many years of bible study, my first spiritual teacher was Burt Harding. From him I learned all the intellectual information necessary to move forward, including fantastic meditation techniques. I also read a tremendous number of books by all kinds of authors and teachers from the far east, and I participated in countless seminars of all types, including several extremely exciting ones. Many, many of them included practices such as fire walking and breaking a sharp arrow on one's throat. Very exhilarating!

I met and studied with many shamans, including Maria Sabina, who was a world-famous witch. Many of these shamans claimed that their heritage went back thousands of years.

I also studied the writings of Buckminster Fuller extensively and attended countless seminars with Drunvalo Melchizedek, who is a "walk-in" with a long lineage of arch angels and beings from ancient Egypt and Greece, including Thoth the Atlantean. From them I have acquired geometrical thinking and extensive knowledge of the workings of the Universe.

I was fortunate enough to study with and be a close friend of Bob Proctor, with whom I met on a weekly basis for 3 years, learning personal growth, leadership and manifestation techniques.

Bob Proctor (left) Edgar Mitchell (middle) Gabor Harsanyi (right)

Another friend I had the rare privilege of having in my life was Captain Edgar Mitchell. He was one of the first men to walk on the moon, and the astronaut with the most spiritual background and interest. I have had many intimate conversations with him, in which I had a chance to question him on topics of a spiritual, yet confidential nature, such as UFO's, the existence of God etc.

Edgar Mitchell (left) and Gabor Harsanyi (right)

After reading and studying all 12 books of the "Earth Chronicles" by Zechariah Sitchin, who after 35 years of extensive research, was able to rewrite human history, I had the great opportunity of being able to study and have extensive discussions with him. I also spent a significant amount of time acquiring knowledge and wisdom from Bruce Lipton, an American developmental biologist, best known for promoting the idea that genes and DNA can be manipulated by a person's beliefs.

Another area I mastered was the Bikram Yoga teachers training course with Bikram Choudhury, who was of the lineage of Bishnu Ghosh, the brother of Parmahansa Yogananda.

Bikram Choudhury (left) Gabor Harsanyi (right)

One of my main teachers was Ramtha the enlightened one, who instilled an amazing amount of spiritual practices and knowledge in me. His lineage goes back to Lemuria, 35,000 years ago, so I suppose the information I have received was from a pretty pure source - this is assuming that the further back we go in time, the purer the source... ha... ha...ha... :)

Some of my practices included countless kundalini experiences, amazing all night meditations and chanting and other astounding, miraculous and colourful encounters. There was a time when the experience in this phase was so magical that I would cry and laugh at the same time for an entire night. I could go on and on... but I think you get the picture!

Kumar: *Wow! That is very impressive. I guess that explains how you were able to achieve your awakening.*

Gabor: *What I have learned from all this gave me a tremendous framework for teaching.* **HOWEVER!!! My acquired knowledge and so-called spiritual experiences had ABSOLUTELY NOTHING to do with awakening.**

I might even say that all the above were rather obstacles to my awakening! If it wasn't for my suicidal depression, I would probably still be engaged in my spiritual studies and pursuits, hoping that sometime in the future I will "arrive" at this mystical point called "enlightenment".

> ## THE VALUE OF ALL MY LEARNINGS WAS IN THE ABRUPT AND INSTANT STOPPING OF IT ALL.

Kumar: *How so? Why do you say obstacle?*

Gabor: *The way we currently learn, which is gathering information, creating mental templates, evaluating, comparing etc. is cumulative in nature and requires continuity. This is very useful to us in our worldly life. After all, if we are learning how to play a violin, it is good to know which master we are learning from, and whether the quality of the violin used is equal to a Stradivarius or one of a lesser quality. In university, it makes a difference where our professor went to school. It makes a difference in the pedigree of our dog and of the breeding of our horse.*

Hence, the human mind assumes that we can somehow get to God accumulatively as well. In other words, we can achieve enlightenment by adding more and more information and good experiences, even from past generations. And thus, we have the notion that God is a higher frequency or a higher octave, and our pursuit should be one of "let's ascend to the light!" or "let's accumulate more and more light credits!" etc. If all this was so, and this assumption was correct, then the "spiritual lineage" concept would be of great importance.

> The same approach that works so well in worldly success, absolutely does not work towards awakening.

*Like most people, I have applied the same discipline, mind-set, and most importantly, the same **approach** to spirituality as I have applied to business and many other successful endeavours in my life. It made sense at that time. Since my approach to business gave me the results I wanted, why shouldn't it be the same in spirituality? So, automatically, I followed the same methods and attitudes – accumulating more and more* *information, knowledge, experiences and good feelings. This, however was my BIG misunderstanding.*

And, of course, I later found out, through blood, sweat, tears, depression, loss of family and friends and all my wealth – that the same approach that worked so well in worldly success, absolutely does not work towards awakening.

> The "continuity" of learning from all the wonderful and impressive teachers had to be abruptly, shockingly and dramatically INTERRUPTED... for me to ever be able to even get close to awakening.
> Ha ha... of course, one can not possibly get "close" to awakening!!! That would be linear progression.

WHOA!!! STOP!!!

From the awakening perspective, the **abrupt and sudden loss** of wealth, family, friends and everything else was the useful point, not the success. In the same manner, the immediate and sharp stopping of my spiritual studies, along with the continuous acquisition of knowledge and experiences, was of great value.

It is absolutely essential for you to get that the thought, "I must have similar extensive experiences", will immunize you against awakening, and will send you in the wrong direction. Please understand that the "instant stopping" can be experienced NOW... at this very moment! My life story has nothing whatsoever to do with your life story. And, yes, you can go on studying in interesting schools and accumulate all kinds of experiences, but to some extend this would mean that you are working against your awakening, since you would be adding more "continuity" which would have to be interrupted vigorously for you to have a chance at awakening.

The more you continue with the continuation of study and accumulation of spiritual knowledge, the harder it will be to bring about the necessary halt that is ultimately required. It would be like trying to stop a train that is in full speed.

Please understand that you don't even need to leave the station!!!

Acquiring more and more information and knowledge, even (or especially) if it is spiritual, is all part of the "Aha Gates" domain. This is where the mind that is still in control is consistently being seduced by the temporary thrill of its realizations, spiritual experiences, epiphanies and what it considers to be "higher states of mind". What is necessary in order to awaken and transcend this old habit is the "Golden Ratio Gate", where the educated taxi can finally drop its false identity and realize that it can take off like a rocket.

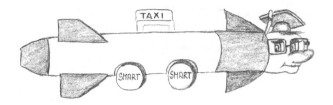

THE LAUNCHING PAD

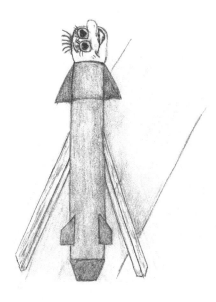

THE "GOLDEN RATIO GATE"
THE ENTRANCE INTO "HOME"

THE "GOLDEN RATIO GATE" AT THE 4TH PROGRESSION

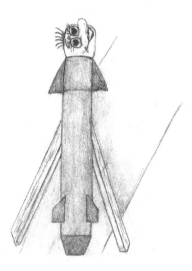

The "Golden Ratio Gate" is a crucial part of this book. It will, therefore, be explained and illustrated in several ways. In preparation for further insights, it is wise to read this section several times.

How Did We Get So Screwed Up?

Question by Michael: *I have studied with many shamans and have been involved with plenty of new age teachers. I have been on a search for so long and I would like to get some understanding of how we got so lost in the first place?! What happened that made us so screwed-up?*

Gabor: *Well, I don't really know for sure, but I will offer my opinion. This subject is best to address and understand from the point of view of the distinction between the primary and the secondary creations, and the*

"Returning Home" of the prodigal son. I will explain what those creations are all about. My intent here is not to lecture you about creation and the universe. I also have no proof of what I am going to say. However, for the sake of making some points very clear, it would be easier to draw you a picture of what I understand - based on my experience - the creation to be.

The primary creation is characterized by "Being" – being of equal proportions to God or the Universe or the Supreme Self, whatever you want to call IT. The Universe was not created in a linear manner, but rather in a logarithmic spiral fashion and with a ratio of 1 to 1.61. The human body, as well as every measurement, expansion and growth in nature, is based on this ratio, also known as the golden ratio.

Nature's numbering system is called the Fibonacci numbers. This is how nature builds, as was discovered by Italian mathematician, Fibonacci. These numbers are: 1, 2, 3, 5, 8, 13, 21, 34, 55, 89, 144... etc. Starting from number "5" there is a ratio of 1.61 between all these numbers. This ratio goes to infinity. It's easy to remember these numbers, since all you have to do is add two consecutive numbers to get to the next one.

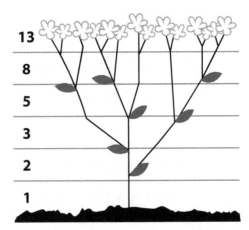

They appear everywhere in nature, from the leaf arrangement in plants, to the pattern of the florets of a flower, to the bracts of a pinecone or to the scales of a pineapple. The Fibonacci numbers are therefore, applicable to the growth of every living thing, including a single cell, a *grain of wheat, a hive of bees, all animals and even all of mankind. If you take a look at your arm, you will see that you have eight fingers in total, five digits on each hand, three bones in each finger, two bones in one thumb, and one thumb on each hand. Your forearm is 1.6 the size of your hand. And on and on it goes...*

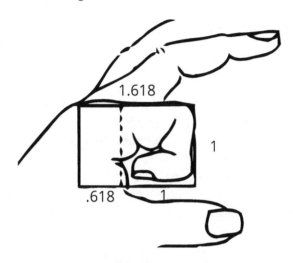

Prior to the first creation, there were no distinctions. Let's take a simple example – imagine that God, which is everything, is yellow. Nothing else exists, with the exception of yellow. If everything is yellow, the first thing that God would have to create out of itself would be "not yellow". God would have to limit itself in order to get to know itself. Once there is something that is "not yellow", there is a distinction that provides a reference point. From that reference point the base of existence is created using the golden ratio. The original distinction in creation is not a frequency. It is a ratio. Everything is created in the same ratio. The NOTHING creates a reference point, and the distinction between the NOTHING and the something becomes the ratio.

> **The original distinction in creation is not a frequency. It is a ratio.**

Duality, also known as the secondary creation, sprung out as a thought from the original reference point of creation. The original ratio was disregarded and derivative thoughts attached themselves to the first linear thought. This created the thought stream that we call duality. It is creation by the mind, and we recognize differences between things through our limited sense at the expense of our "unifying ability". From this we built the interface of our current reality that is strictly based on our sense perceptions and everything has to make "sense". This is really nonsense! Since 99% of reality is unperceivable by our senses, there is a lot more "non-sense" than "sense".

In the original creation, there is ratio recognition. The Creator forms a reference point from which it can recognize itself, and that outer reference is produced as a ratio. Hence, the ratio recognition is created. God (so to speak) "creates his children in His own image" meaning, in His/Her own proportions. Something is generated from NOTHING, and in order to measure itself, a ratio is created. This can be called the Father/Mother God, which decided to send out parts of Itself to have further experiences.

Michael: *Experiences of what?*

Gabor: *Of "I AM That." "I AM That out there too." God's children are the same ratio as God, only "smaller", so to speak. God divided himself into small pieces of the same ratio (see fractals) – "As within, so without!" Now we have "mini-Gods" – God's children – "US" ... made in the same proportions as the Creator, just smaller. Now we can co-create with God just like we were fashioned.*

Since creation equals referencing, we are allowed to easily create from the reference point of proportions. We need a reference point to create from, and when we do so from the point of the same ratio used by the Creator, it is called co-creating.

> **For co-creation, we have all the equipment necessary – a body, the ability to pay attention and the capability to make sound and words.**

We have all the equipment necessary – a body (which bears the same ratio), the ability to pay attention (which is a God-like ability) and the capability to make sounds and words. We have a built-in ratio from which creation is possible. Hence, we have to create in the same fashion as our Father/Mother Creator... from the reference point of ratios. This is what the Golden Age was like - a period of primordial peace, harmony, stability, and prosperity.

Before the secondary creation brought about duality, the subdivided little Gods happily co-created with the big Creator, and everyone had the recognition of Oneness with God and all of creation. There was always an automatic inner focus. Jesus had ratio recognition. That's how he was able to say, "I and my Father are One."

The little Gods were also given the ability to choose and think, which made the distinction between humans and animals. The intent of giving the choice ability did not include the use of this ability to alter the original ratio imbedded within. However, the ability to choose has been **misused**. *This mismanagement came in the form of moving away from the ratio of*

> We used our God-given ability to choose to alter the basic ratio of existence! Hence duality emerged.

the Creator and producing a separate creation, that is not compatible with God's ratio of creation.

This was the fall of man. We used our God-given ability to choose to alter the basic ratio of existence, hence duality emerged. The new creation is separated by its own referencing that is no longer in keeping with our origin as Being created in God's image.

> **In the secondary creation, we started to use our own linear referencing system, which is not in keeping with our origin, as beings created in God's image.**

As we continued to create in this fashion, using our mind's dualistic nature without the support or the reference to the original Creator, many duality-based derivatives were produced in the thought stream such as: "good-bad", "right-wrong", "happy-sad", "spiritual-secular", "absolute-relative" etc. This is the linear creation and we have been on this road a long time.

Being representatives of God, we are meant to go out and discover new things while recognizing that "This is me too, as I am One with the Creator." As we started to alter the base ratio, we began to create linear realities or sub-realities which too are God, since everything is, but this is no longer based on the original ratio that the Creator would be able to recognize and call his child. We created a new base that God does not recognize and we have done this for so long that we now have a new and different reality. This reality is nothing but a pseudo-reality, or a corrupted version of the original reality. Time was created by adding linearity to a non-linear existence.

For the purpose of language, we are calling this "mis-creating". We go on and keep mis-creating and this becomes what is known as karma, because linearity is in the realm of time and cause and effect. As long as we remain unconscious (which is the false ratio) we can hypothetically go on forever trying to find our way Home, by attempting to clean up our karma with good deeds and spirituality, but to no avail since the original ratio is still not being engaged.

On the other hand, when we do wake up and become conscious, all the fake reference points and false ratios take a back seat, because in being conscious and awake to our inner being, we are actually realigning ourselves to our original ratio. This is in keeping with God's original creation. And this is actually extremely simple. Our bodies are the perfect temples that can facilitate this awakening, since they are in the exact ratio, as is all creation.

By simply turning our attention inside and feeling the inner vitality of the body, we are literally knocking on the door in order to go through the "Golden Ratio Gate" and enter into the creator's kingdom. Once we enter here, God can now recognize us as his own image and likeness and we are HOME.

> **As long as we remain unconscious, we can hypothetically go on forever trying to find our way Home, by attempting to clean up our karma with good deeds and spirituality, but to no avail since the original ratio is still not being engaged.**

> **Being representatives of God, we are meant to go out and discover new things while recognizing, "This is me too, as I am One with the Creator!"**

So, What is the "Golden Ratio Gate"?

As mentioned earlier, since the "Golden Ratio Gate" is such a major part of this book, I will explain and illustrate it in several ways. There is a lot of information coming your way but I assure you that if you re-read this chapter several times before moving on to the following chapters, the information will land on you in many different ways and open you up to further realizations and ready you for advanced awakening techniques. Let's first take a look at the "Golden Ratio Gate" & 4th Progression chart 1. below.

The Golden Ratio Gate

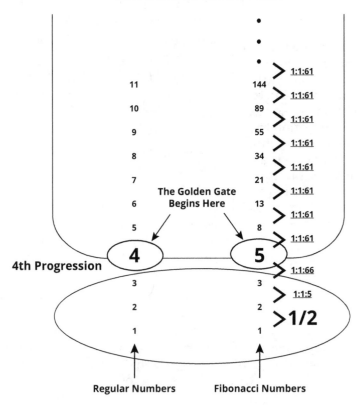

The "Golden Ratio Gate" and the 4th Progression – Chart 1.

You will notice a column of regular progressive numbers on the left. These are linear numbers. The next column of numbers to the right of the regular numbers, is made up of progressing Fibonacci numbers. On the right side of the latter column are the ratios between the numbers as they progress.

If you look at the bottom right, where the Fibonacci number "1" progresses on to "2", you will see "1/2" written to the right, between the "1" and the "2".

2

➢ 1/2

1

This signifies that at this point there is still no real Fibonacci ratio. When there was just "1" and no other, "1" did not have an identity or an existence of its own. Since there was nothing else but "1", the "1" was actually **ONENESS**. As soon as "2" showed up, "1" began to exist as an entity on to itself, since it now had a reference point that was other than itself - the "2". So, the first ratio creation is not really a ratio, but rather a division into two - "1" divided itself into two halves. At this point the "2" came into existence, since now "1" turned into a number from **ONENESS** and therefore the ratio is "1/2".

When we move up from the "2" the ratios begin, but with no consistency, until we reach the 4th progression – "4" in the regular numbers column, and "5" in the Fibonacci column. (see below) Here the ratios are 1:1.61 and we find a consistency in them.

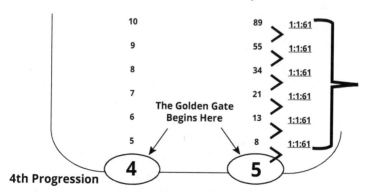

This is very significant. This is the shift to the Fibonacci ratio - the shift from inconsistency to consistency and it continues to infinity. This consistent ratio offers the possibility of a "Golden Ratio Gate" because at any point, not just at the 4th progression, we can enter the world of the golden ratio. The world of the golden ratio reflects the basis of reality, which is consistent, and which we were aware of during the Golden Age.

The fact that no matter where in the chart we want to enter, it is still a world in the same ratio, is indicative of the fact that from here on, this is the world of "sameness". It is the elevated platform in which "sameness" is celebrated. In our linear and dualistic world (below the 4th progression), although we are always seeking consistency where there is none, "differences" are celebrated. Hence, the perpetual habit of comparing and identity seeking. Both modes of operating – the "sameness" as well as the "differences" - are needed. However, we are attempting here to awaken the organ (our body, that is in the golden ratio) that enables us to celebrate "sameness", which heretofore, has not been very fashionable.

Thus, the 4th progression is of the utmost importance. Until we become aware of it, our attention is constantly pulled by the attraction to our "smart wheels" and our duality-based identities. It continuously flows out with little to no interest in going within. Once we become aware of the significance of the 4th progression, we realize that this is where our attention must be directed to, if we are to awaken and live from an elevated platform of being. For this reason, from this point on, the remaining focus of this book and everything we say or do, is measured by how useful it is in bringing our attention to this fundamental and critical point – the 4th progression.

At this place, that we are calling the 4th progression, there is no longer a linear progression. Here there is no progression, but a "leap". Although from the 4th progression on we can enter the "Golden Ratio Gate" or the golden ratio reality, we cannot "continue" into it. We must "leap" out of the contrast-reality into the 4th progression at an angle. This is a point of leaping, angling, surrendering. This is where the mind begins to acquire its angling abilities, and this is what all our practices are based on. (see "Angular Leap" graph below)

At the 4th progression there is no longer a linear progression. There is only a "leap". We cannot "continue" into it but rather, "leap" into it. We must "leap" out of the contrast-reality into the 4th progression at an angle.

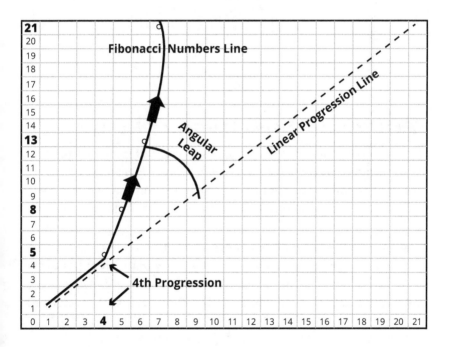

"Angular Leap" – Illustrated by Fibonacci numbers plotted on a graph

ATTENTION...IS THE MAGICAL KEY TO THE "GOLDEN RATIO GATE"

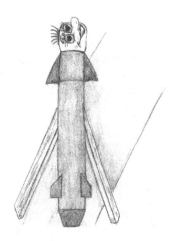

"First Hand" or "Hand-Me-Down" Reality?

There are more "Golden Ratio Gate" chart illustrations to come, as I promised, to offer various explanations. However, I would first like to introduce a very important consideration that will shed even more light on this most significant topic. It has to do with attention and language.

It has been proven by many experiments that when we observe a stream of light, it behaves differently, depending on our attention on it. When we look with expectation - i.e. with mind involvement - the stream of light becomes a particle. However, when we are not observing with our mind – by either not looking at all, or by observing consciously – the same stream of light is seen as a wave.

Our attention is our biggest asset!!!

It is also a known fact that attention follows language and attention also leads consciousness and energy. In our current state of thinking, or should I say, "being thought" by the "smart wheels", it would be quite accurate to say that 99% of our attention is placed within the "smart wheels". It is pulled there and kept locked in by our duality-based language. This is one of the main contributors to the kind of consciousness (or lack thereof) that is being experienced on the planet these days. Recognizing this as a crucial element in our need for transformation, would it not make sense that the language we use must be investigated as well?

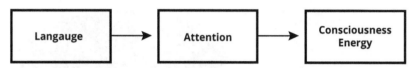

Entering through the "Golden Ratio Gate" is entering into the realm of Silence, or what we call the "Elevated Platform of Living", which is in the domain of the golden ratio. In this phase, it is almost impossible to find the right words to use. The language of the 3rd dimension is limiting by design. In an attempt to teach that which is beyond the mind, many mind-based words have sprung up in order to describe the indescribable. Even those who have had awakenings have to leave the elevated space and return to the 3rd dimension for the purpose of explanation.

The problem is that these words have been over used, mis-used and abused to the point that now, when used, they are not capable of being pointers to Silence. In fact, they do nothing but prompt the listener/seeker to visit his or her own spiritual template store house. This is where a memory is pulled out and compared, and another mental conclusion is arrived at with the accompanying "aha" intellectual satisfaction - assuming that a new understanding has been arrived at.

For example, when the word "silence" is used, one may immediately pull out thoughts of meditation, a serene forest, a religious experience, etc., depending on his or her accumulated spiritual templates.

Many spiritual teachers have also begun to borrow terms from other languages, especially from Sanskrit, which has been the "in" spiritual language for many years. These too have been over used and even twisted in their meanings to suit the Western culture. For example, the Sanskrit word "Avatar" means, "a manifestation of a deity or released soul in bodily form on earth; an incarnate divine teacher". However, it is now used also as "an icon or figure representing a particular person in a computer game".

Lord Krishna, a Real Avatar   Computer Avatar

Advertisers have also started bastardizing spiritual phrases. For example, the phrase "Be here now!" is used in some ads that are written on the walls of a fast-food restaurant.

So, let me remind you: energy and consciousness follow attention. Language directs our attention and, in turn, guides our energy and consciousness. We need expressions and words to convey precisely where the attention should go. With inaccurate or false use of language our life is lived in a false "hand-me-down" reality.

Consciousness Follows Attention.
Attention Leads Consciousness.

Is the World Still Flat?

We frequently use the words "up" and "down". It seems quite innocent, but those are left-over words from medieval times, when the world was perceived as, and believed to be, flat. Of course, now we know that everything is in constant movement – the earth is spinning around its own axis, and it also revolves around the sun.

So, from our observer perspective, we are actually seeing around the curvature of the earth, and that is not a straight line. (Perhaps this is what Einstein meant by "curved space".) Yet, the concept of "up" and "down" stuck with us from our ignorance days, and we follow this by using expressions like: "Move up in the world", or "I am feeling really down today", or "We need to go up to a higher level of consciousness." – all of which have become obstacles to awakening.

If good is always indicated by moving "up" and bad is referred to as going "down" – where does our attention go immediately when the words "up" or "down" are mentioned? This habit has become ingrained in us to the point of oblivion. Thus, when we are asked to go within, we are not at all comfortable or familiar with this.

> With respect to attention, I don't think that most people are aware that it is one of our biggest and most essential assets!

Our attention on a stream of light, which is the basic ingredient of our material world, can make the light appear as a particle or as a wave. So, bottom line – if our attention is so powerful that it can change the light from a wave to a particle, it is evident that the attention has to be directed correctly, in order to "master" our reality. Certainly, advertisers know the value of our attention. They are extremely successful in directing it.

(As always, the outside references mentioned in this book are only brought up as sub-notes and it is not absolutely necessary to understand them. There is plenty of information on this on the internet if you wish to seek further.)

Cosmically Inaccurate Language Leads to Catastrophic Consequences!

What it is essential to understand is: since language governs our attention and our attention directs energy and consciousness – error in language usage can and does have catastrophic consequences when it comes to awakening, which is the subject of this book. This is not an exaggeration! The use of language has been so cosmically inaccurate... no wonder so few are waking up. We have become so used to this that we innocently accept this as being ok, even though we consistently mis-create because of this. So the question is, how can cosmically inaccurate language lead us onto the platform of unifying consciousness?

An Ancient Language – Not Just a Pointer!

There is however, an ancient language that I am familiar with, that is very close in nature to the source from which it has originated, and many of its words act as exceptional pointers which not only provide the appropriate feeling of essence, but also include the way to access it. These words have special qualities inherently expressed in them. This language has been totally mis-understood in its every day use – however it has not yet been bastardised by intellectual spirituality.

Actually, I am calling them "pointers" here as a bridge to get the true significance of these words. They are much more than pointers. They are the actual representation of the essence that we are attempting to speak of and from.

An Ancient Language - Decoded & Reloaded

Although these words are used in common language, they can be decoded by one who is present, thus bringing out their inherent essential meaning. The scholars of this ancient language wouldn't necessarily know its true significance, since the deeper implication of its words is only gotten when the "decrypting from within is activated". Many people prefer to keep this a secret and let it remain in the realm of mystery, but my sense is that the meaning and the decoding of ancient languages belong to everyone, especially since they offer a deeper meaning and access to the "Golden Ratio Gate".

A "Star Seed" Language with Retained Original Value

The ancient language that contains the main criteria for picking a transcendent one is Magyar (pronounced 'madge-yar'). The word "Mag" means "seed". Using my poetic license, I would say that Magyar is a "Star Seed language", because of the obvious value system it contains. In Magyar, the word for wealth or value is "vagyon" (pronounced vadjyon), and it actually means "Beingness".

So, I picked this language to assist in the understanding of the full significance of the "Golden Ratio Gate". It is a great gift to be able to use a language that has retained the golden ratio orientation... a language in which the value system it is founded on, is not one of fear-based survival and the loosening up of chains. Thus, there is no doubt in my mind that it is an accurate and befitting language to support my attempts to offer explanations on a topic that is beyond duality verbiage.

Therefore, I will be introducing a few terms from Magyar in this book, starting with this chapter, in order to build a new foundation for you, the readers. It is a stepping stone that will allow you to re-direct your attention. This will in turn, assist you in waking up to the elevated platform, to have a smooth entry through the "Golden Ratio Gate" and to be able to integrate this new space in your day-to-day lives through practice. This will also help you to internalize the meaning and at the same time, erase the disadvantage of the written word, since by the time it is written it is already "not now"/the past and therefore, some of the potency is lost.

Bread Crumbs to Find Our Way HOME!

This ancient language has retained the reference to space, or the unknown, as well as our relationship to the unknown. It has kept the bread crumbs that are dispersed along the path so that we can find our way HOME. Here and there, throughout history, there have been attacks on this language. There have been attempts to destroy it and to take the wisdom and spaciousness out of it. However, since this language is universally coded, the essence of it is indestructible.

Some of the words of this ancient language have become the cornerstones of the heart and core of this chapter. Please don't get hung up on this. The only reason it is being introduced and used in this fashion is because ancient languages emerged at a time when we were all ONE. The essence of this coded language is **ONENESS** and it originated before separation took place. I took some liberties in my interpretations and I employ some poetic licence since the goal here is not verbal accuracy, but rather clear, easy and effortless awakening.

Who Left the Key in the Gate?

In the ancient language of Magyar, the "Golden Gate" is called "***Arany Kapu***" (pronounced 'aran-kapoo'). By adding an apostrophe-like sign on top of the second "a", we get "***Arány Kapu***", which means "Golden Ratio Gate". It is the Golden Gate, which also means that it is the "Golden Ratio Gate". The ratio itself contains the key as to the "how to" - how to open the gate and access HOME. This is an example of a phrase that has the meaning as well as the "how to" included in it. In this case, the name "Golden Ratio Gate" itself means that someone has left the key in it. This will become clearer very soon. I promise!

From Intellectuality to Intelligence

Awakening is the unification of man with intelligent cosmic forces. Since our lives have so far been based on the contrast-based limitation of intellectuality, intelligence seems to be the key missing ingredient. We have been trying to resolve all our life's problems intellectually - "intell-***actually***" - which is content-based, where as intelligence - "intell-*igen*-ce" - is context-based. The Magyar word "***Igen***" (pronounced 'eeg-en'), which in day-to-day life means "yes", is included, as you can see, in the word "intell-***igen***-ce".

Intelligence seems to be the key missing ingredient.

"Igen" is a coded word that is carried forth in the Magyar language. In its coded format, it is a seed word or a central word, very much like the cog of a wheel, from which all kinds of essential truths are derived. It offers, as you will soon see, the beginning of a new world that once entered, presents the possibility of true intelligence.

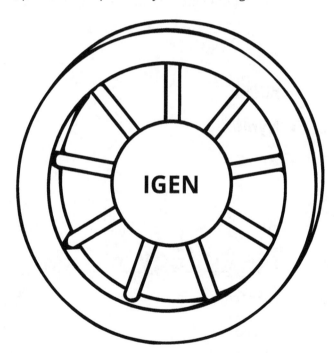

Why is the "Igen" so important? The "Igen" is connected to two other very significant words: "***Egy***" (pronounced 'edge') which means one or ***ONENESS;*** and "Négy" (pronounced 'neidge'), which means "four". In this coded language of Magyar, which can be read backward and forward, "igen" read backward becomes "***negy***" (the "Y" and the "I" in this context are interchangeable.), which contains the "egy".

IGEN

NEGI

I = Y   NEGI ⟶ NÉGY

In these numbers - egy (1) and negy (4) - it clearly shows that we need to pay attention to the "four", since that's where the word "Igen" makes its return home through the elevation of the "***egy***" (one) to "n***egy***" (four) by adding the letter 'n.' (See chart of Magyar numbers below)

10 • **Tiz**

9 • **Kilenc**

8 • **Nyolc**

7 • **Hét**

6 • **Hat**

5 • **Öt**

4 • **<u>Négy (Egy +n)</u>**

3 • **Három**

2 • **Kettő**

1 • **<u>Egy</u>**

Intelligence: The Key Pointer to the 4th Progression

Oneness in the language returns as the "four", which is the place where the major shift takes place and the consistency of the golden ratio begins. The great significance of "**Igen**" shows up at the 4th progression, which is the point where the prodigal son returns HOME. This is also the place where the power of the "Igen" is revealed once again, as we move into the world of "intell-IGEN-ce" and transcend the duality of "intel-actuality" (As is shown in the chart).

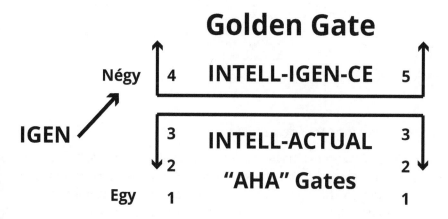

It is important to note that the section of the "Intell-Actual" is where the "Aha Gates" reside.

The great significance of "Igen" shows up as part of
"intell-igen-ce" at the 4th progression.
This is the point where the prodigal son
finally returns HOME.

4th PROGRESSION –
GEOMETRICAL PERSPECTIVE

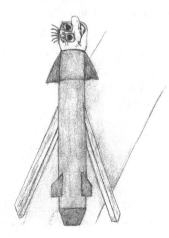

The Triality Perspective

Not to worry, I have no intentions of offering a lecture on geometry. Nonetheless, there are a few geometric concepts that contribute to the appreciation, understanding and significance of the "Golden Ratio Gate" and humanity's need to awaken. Let's take another look at the "Golden Ratio Gate" chart. This time we will examine the "Golden Ratio Gate" and 4th Progression (chart 2.), as it contains the corresponding geometrical shapes as they appear in the 4th progression.

The Golden Ratio Gate

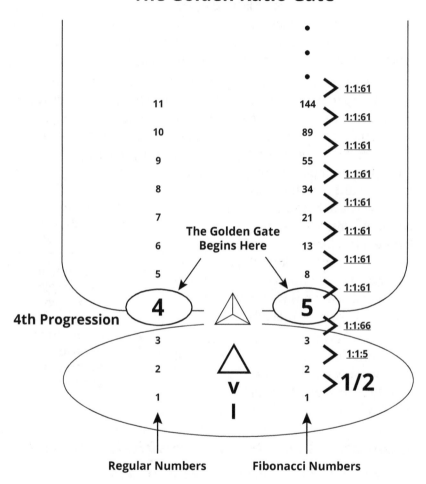

The "Golden Ratio Gate" and the 4th Progression - Chart 2.

You will notice in the center of this chart, there are four geometric shapes from number "1" to the 4th progression. These represent the progressive numbers by containing the corresponding number of lines connecting the vertices. As you can see, to the right of the number "1" there is a plain line - **I**; by the "2" there is the **V** which has two lines; by the "3" there is a triangle that, obviously, has 3 lines - △. The triangle represents humanity's attempts to fix or equalize the chaos and confusion that are created in duality.

It has become a somewhat ignored yet normal feeling within most individuals, that something is always off. We try to eliminate this discomfort by attempting to build life with as much sustaining power, consistency and steadiness as possible. We are forever struggling to secure the structural integrity of the many various mental and emotional templates that we have accumulated over the years, and upon which we have based our value systems and identities. We attempt to solve the inherent problems created by duality with an equalizer line, thus creating the triangle. The triangle is structurally stable because it has structural integrity, yet it contains no enclosed space.

> We are forever struggling to secure the structural integrity of the many various mental and emotional templates that we have accumulated over the years, and upon which we have based our value systems and identities.

It also represents life as a triality. In spiritual circles, there is a lot of talk about duality, but we mostly live in a world of "triality". For example, "black, white and grey", or "hot, cold and lukewarm".

Attempting to Destroy Chaos with More Chaos!

The triangle is also used to represent the destruction cycle, that we have been following for a long time. For example: there is a crisis in one or several areas in our life; it reaches a critical mass in which we can no longer tolerate the problem; we resolve it in the most common way that we currently tend to default to – chaos and then destruction. For instance, we have problems in our marriage, we reach a point where we cannot tolerate our partner and we resolve our situation by destroying the marriage. See diagram 4.

Personal level

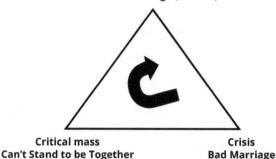

**Violent Solution
End the Marriage (divorce)**

**Critical mass
Can't Stand to be Together**

**Crisis
Bad Marriage**

DIAGRAM 4

The same thing occurs on a global scale. A country has a problem when its economy is bad, it reaches a critical mass when its citizens are starving and the solution that is arrived at is usually war and destruction. See diagram 5.

Global level

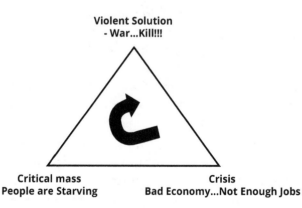

**Violent Solution
- War...Kill!!!**

**Critical mass
People are Starving**

**Crisis
Bad Economy...Not Enough Jobs**

DIAGRAM 5

We believe the destruction triangle to be normal, since we have followed this trail of action for so long. We also have the continuous reinforcement of this thanks to the entertainment industry, which has inundated us with the growing popularity of adventure stories in films and on TV, where conflicts are increasingly resolved by employing blood-shed and violence.

The Tetrahedron – We Are Ready for Take-Off!

The significant point about the 4th progression is that the key point, where we arrive at the 4th progression, is also the place where from a triangle, we "progress" to a tetrahedron, which is the birth of a new way of equalizing and problem solving. This is the realm of cosmic order where there is really nothing to resolve. Here one is connected to the universal flow, since he/she has entered the domain of the golden ratio. P.S. – you have just come HOME! This will be explained in greater depth in the next chapter.

The tetrahedron is the first of the geometric shapes that has an "inside" and an "outside" as it contains "space", while the previous shapes from "1" to "3" or from the triangle down, are all flat.

The fact that the tetrahedron has an "inside" and an "outside", makes it a very good representation of the human ability to shift back to our origin, where "inside" and "outside" are considered, as opposed to the false considerations of "up" and "down". Here we are entering an entirely different world, which is a totally new platform for a human being to operate from. We are entering now into real human transformation.

Please note: We have just transcended the concept of "up" and "down" and brought in the "inside" and "outside" consideration. This an example of evolution of terms. But please don't get too comfortable with this new consideration, because even the concepts of "inside" and "outside" eventually must evolve into a more accurate expression: "convergence" and "divergence". By turning our attention within the body, which is a replica of the universe, we are converging with the universe. When we pull our attention out of that reality and back into the contrast-reality, we are diverging from the universe. This will become clearer as you continue to read.

If we plot the Fibonacci numbers on a graph we will get a spiral. The simplest way to show this is to take our tetrahedron and mark the Fibonacci numbers on its vectors to show not only the spiral, but the spaciousness aspect of it. (See diagram 6. below)

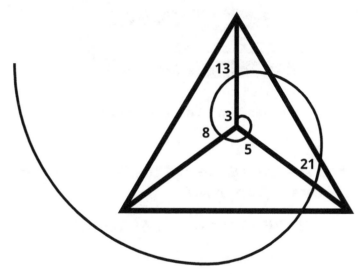

Diagram 6. View from the top

Please don't get too hung up on the geometry. The key here is to get that the spiral indicates the spatial aspect of reality, as opposed to a flat platform. Diagram 7 below shows the same spiral as it is viewed from the side. The purpose of this diagram is to show visually, the relationship between our 3rd dimensional "flat reality" (represented by the x, y and z lines, or the flat triangle above the "13") and the spaciousness of existence itself (represented by the spiral). This existential reality spiral actually weaves through all realities, including our flat one.

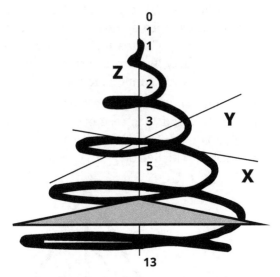

Diagram 7. View from the side

What do the "Aha Gates" & the "Golden Ratio Gate" have in Common?

<u>NOTHING ("no thing") WHATSOEVER!</u>

If the "Aha Gates" and the "Golden Ratio Gate" have nothing whatsoever in common, how can we possibly expect to ascend to the heavens of awakening by using the stairway of the "Aha Gates"?

Diagram 8 below shows the "Aha Gates" and the "Golden Ratio Gate" side by side. The "Aha Gates" are represented by the stairs on the left, and the "Golden Ratio Gate" is represented by the spiral. As you can see, they have nothing in common, even if the "Aha Gates" are spiritually motivated. The "Aha Gates" are all about ascending "up" to higher levels of intellectual understanding and accumulating knowledge, good feelings and behavior patterns, in the hope that these will get one to awaken from a mundane life to a more spiritual one. It is impossible to ever "arrive"!

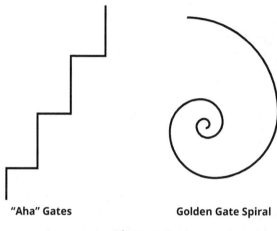

"Aha" Gates   Golden Gate Spiral

Diagram 8.

The "Aha Gates" would make one think that there is higher knowledge... that there is a formula for success... that in order to evolve, there must be a higher vibration, a higher octave or a higher frequency (all kinds of words were invented with such dexterity!). This gave rise to the belief that one must prepare the body and mind for those higher vibrations and octaves, which in turn produced all kinds of "spiritual" practices and rituals such as meditation, diets, fasting, cleansing of the chakras, clearing of emotional cobwebs (as a pre-requisite) and on and on.

This whole kind of approach comes from the "Aha Gates" typical methodology. The proper application of the "Aha Gates" makes our lives "better" albeit not forever, in this dimension. Therefore, we believe that the same approach should work in our attempt to reach God or the Creator.

Somewhere in the human mind it is assumed that there will be some kind of awakening at the end of the road... at a future time. It is a very logical supposition because, thus far, most things have come to us through searching, comparing, shopping around, etc. - and most importantly, these all came in "time". As the old saying goes, "Good things come to those who wait." A very much "time-based" statement that we have all heard and adopted so reverently.

In the "Aha Gates" everything is in the future, and things have to be improved upon consistently in order to jump to the next more advanced level. All the efforts to have more refine frequencies, higher vibrations, purer bodies and minds, more releasing of emotions and beliefs, more peeling of the onion, more, more, more... etc. etc. All these point to an accumulation that leads to a future event. Sometime in the future we will be refined enough, purified enough... and only then we will reach God.

There are many "Aha Steps" one can ascend to "progressively" and many "Aha Gates" to enter in time. This is akin to the belief that there are many roads that lead to God. However, there is only ONE "Golden Ratio Gate" and this is where "progression", "continuity", and "time" come to an end. This is the "Angular Leap", the direct, instant and permanent union with our creator that can only occur at the present moment.

All the mysticism engulfing this whole subject acts as a pacifier and a lure to a future event. This makes a lot of logical sense to the current mind, which is consistently seeking improvement and a better life. For real and permanent awakening out of the 3rd dimension, all the above "Aha" approaches and tactics are obsolete. They are guaranteed not to work since it is the "Golden Ratio Gate" that we have to go through in order to awaken.

WARNING

LAUNCHING ERROR!

ROCKET WITH TAXI MENTALITY

SIRENS AT THE GATES

The Spiritual Gate-keepers

So far, we have talked about the "Aha Gates" and how the mind works within its "smart wheels" with all its accumulated templates and values that form its identity. We then looked at the "Golden Ratio Gate" which is the "Golden World" we need to become aware of as an underlying base or platform, that spirals through all existence and which is interwoven with all living realities. The terms "Golden World" and "Golden Ratio Gate" are interchangeable. The "Golden Ratio Gate" access is available absolutely at anytime and anywhere, and therefore, we don't make a distinction between the "Golden Ratio Gate" and the "Golden World" that it opens up to.

> The "Golden Ratio Gate" is the world we need to become "aware" of as an underlying base, that spirals through all existence. It is interwoven like a magic carpet with all living realities.

Many of us have heard time and again phrases such as "it is all within", "the truth, or what we are searching for is already here!" etc. In as much as these statements are true, they have been bastardized through repetition and intellectual assertions without the backing of true understanding and awareness and without the "how to" guidance through this major shift. And although this has been intellectually satisfying, in our hearts we know that it is just not enough, since "going within" is never achieved by the contrast-based mind or intellect.

The Truth that we are seeking truly does already exist. It never was not in existence, but unlike the intellectual approach in the "Aha Gates", the "Golden Ratio Gate" cannot be approached in the same fashion with time-based accumulating knowledge.

The only appropriate approach to awakening is anti-accumulating, anti-continuity... It is a "stopping" and a collapsing into presence by turning within and becoming aware of ever-present existence. The present moment is just that – the present moment. It is not a continuation of the previous moment with its accumulated impressions and

> The present moment is not a continuation of the previous moment with its accumulated impressions and thought streams.

thought streams. This must be demonstrated and lived in one's every day experience, and not just "talked about".

At this point I will get into one of the most important milestones of this book. I call it the "Sirens at the Gates". The Sirens were beautiful but dangerous creatures. According to Greek mythology, they lured the sailors with their beautiful voices to their doom, causing the ships to crash on the reefs near their island. A well-known encounter is described in the Odyssey. Odysseus plugged the crew's ears with wax and ordered them to bind him on the mast of the ship. He also told them that no matter how much he begged, they must not untie him. When they passed near the Sirens' island, Odysseus started begging his shipmates to let him go, but none heard him.

In the spiritual world, the Sirens are forever lurking at the "Aha Gates", waiting to ambush us and sabotage our possibility of awakening, by pretending to offer improvements to our existing contrast-reality.

> **Improving on contrast-reality is still contrast-reality!**

The Sirens are those points along the way, where we get lured and conned by paths, teachings or practices that are outer, shinier, more mysterious, more spiritual-sounding, more intellectual, more reputable, more fashionable, more dogmatic, etc. - all of which act as Sirens who call you sweetly and pull you and your attention to their dangerous domain – the intellectual "Aha Gates" type of modalities. They ensure that we never really turn within. They all sound so good and so spiritual, as they fill our heads with partial truths.

> **Partial truths are not partially useful. Just as a vaccine has a bit of the disease injected into us to immunize us against a disease, a partial truth immunizes us against awakening to the truth.**

Many of them even throw in words like "going within", "the now", "awakening", which sound marvelous and feel like the right thing. However, when these words are uttered via the intellect and out of context, they totally immunize the bedazzled seeker against awakening. This is because, by the time they hear the same words from the elevated platform of the "Golden Ratio Gate", most seekers have already heard them before, and therefore they immediately invalidate and dismiss them as "Oh... I already know this!" not realizing that this "knowing" is purely intellectual. Here again we see that the principle of "continuity" that we are so accustomed to in the 3rd dimension guarantees complete failure when it comes to awakening.

The Sirens appear as organizations, methodologies and individuals that participate in the spiritual supermarket and they serve up their own version of well packaged spirituality. Currently, the mind is run by the "smart wheels" of the "Aha Gates". Therefore, in order to lure you in, the Sirens, in their unconscious state, use the well-oiled recognition system that has been developed by the interactive mental faculties.

The biggest ERROR caused by the Sirens is in preventing one from recognizing that the "Aha Gates" and the "Golden Ratio Gate" have nothing whatsoever in common. They attempt to help us ascend to the heavens via the stairway of the "Aha Gates", just as a rocket would try to ascend while maintaining the taxi mentality!

There is a direct path to God and it is like a bridge over a huge gorge. The Sirens' job is to distract one from taking the straight line that goes directly to God. They consistently seduce seekers to go the long, circuited way that never gets there, but down to the gorge, where it is nice and cozy. And then... if they still have a shred of motivation left for change, these semi-dormant seekers are faced with climbing up the steep slope of the gorge. All the while, the spiritual templates fanned by the Sirens, are whispering in their heads, "Please stay down here with us. You have become so spiritually advanced." So, back down the chasm most seekers go, defending their spiritual identity that the Sirens have graciously bestowed upon them. It is high time to become like Odysseus.

Thus, the Sirens gain momentum and power and the result is: "The Gorge Maintainers Association"

made up of the top Sirens, who feed on the main mental activities of the "smart wheels" of the "Aha Gates" and make one believe that "perceived improvements" in life equal awakening. Remember diagram 3 from the "Aha Gates" chapter? (see below)

Could perceived improvements in life possibly equal awakening???

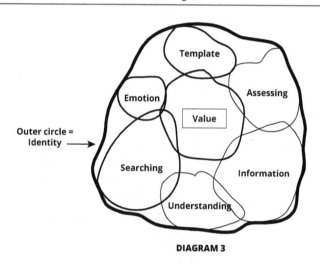

DIAGRAM 3

To spice things up, many of these packages also include mystery in the form of unusual and extraordinary ceremonies and teachers wearing different costumes while sitting on a throne... totally removed from the "little spiritual people". This fills the templates with the identity of "I am a sincere spiritual seeker, well connected in the spiritual arena and I accept this mysterious path, even though my teacher is so high up there that it seems totally unachievable. So, that's good, since I will be doing this for a long time and everything worthwhile takes a long time. This way I will be proving that I am worthy, since I never give up. Thus my identity and values will be kept alive. And of course, I continuously practice humility and surrender at the feet of my guru."

Now those templates have a lot of new knowledge, information and spiritual emotions to assess and analyse, but nothing new has really happened. They are still the old templates, thinking they have advanced, since they have acquired new content. The problem is that the templates are still the same, and very few seem to be aware of this.

My father visited me in Canada in the early 90's, shortly after the collapse of communism in Eastern Europe. I asked him one morning, as we were sipping our coffee, "What has changed in Hungary now that it is no longer under the communist regime?" To my surprise, my father said, "Not much. The bed-sheets have been changed, but the prostitutes remained the same."

This is what happens when we eat the spiritual delicacies that the Sirens serve us. The food may be spicier but the plates/templates are the same... and therefore, there is no transformation. Nor can there possibly be any hope of awakening into an elevated platform of being. The food on the plate (the content) may change but unless the plate itself (the context) changes, nothing happens. No amount of improvement on the food will make a difference here. For a real transformation to take place, there must be a contextual shift, which will be explained in great detail in the upcoming chapters.

Watching TV – A Modern Day Yogic Practice?

Question by Zoltan Horvat: *Some teachers warn against certain obstacles. For example, they say that watching TV will pollute your mind. What are your thoughts about this?*

Gabor: *The concept of "not watching TV" comes from the perspective that we should not pollute our mind. It is based on the assumption that for an unpolluted mind it is easier to achieve enlightenment. This approach is cumulative in style and belongs to the "personal growth" category in which we start at a point of improving ourselves someway, changing our behavior patterns and accumulating good deeds and positive thinking, with the hope that one day in the future - preferably the "far" future - there will be more "time" for keeping up the search and the new identity it provides... that one day in the future, we will have the right vibration or the right frequency with a purified body and great practiced behavior. That's when, for sure, we will earn the right to get closer and closer to God... and in turn, achieve enlightenment... ha, ha, ha!*

The skill that you will be learning in my next seminar, is one that enables you to "bypass" the mind entirely. Making the mind "heavier" or "lighter" does not matter. Making it "lighter" does not relate to enlightenment... it is not on the same page, not in the same book and not even in the same library! We are not keen on "fall-on-your-ass" prevention techniques. We are interested in elevating the floor! So, where the power is, is totally in the "bypassing" of the mind.

> **We are not keen on "fall-on-your-ass prevention" techniques!**
>
> **We are interested in elevating the floor!**

By "bypassing" I don't mean ignoring or shoving it under the carpet. It is rather a turning within and dealing with things from an inner bodily elevated platform, with no mind interference, adjudication or evaluation. We practice "bypassing" systems and NOT "lighten-the-load" systems.

(Note to readers: see more on this in the "Forget-me-not Definitions" chapter at the end of the book.)

And, by the way, I know this will sound weird, but watching TV – even violent programs – is one of the exercises that we practice in the advanced stage of the integration part of awakening.

The power is in the "bypassing" of the mind!

Zoltan: *Really? How so?*

Gabor: *Once you understand that we are "bypassing" and not accumulating, you will see that being able to "bypass" the mind's reaction to a violent scene, is in itself a desired ability of the elevated platform of being. If I can "bypass" a template that triggers strong emotions, by watching conflict and aggression on TV, then it would stand to reason that my "bypassing" abilities will be enhanced.*

Relationships - Coagulated Misery or Fast Track to Awakening?

Zoltan: *And what about being in a relationship? Some teachers warn that being in a relationship will slow your progress down.*

Gabor: *A relationship is the best ongoing seminar for the Western mind. It provides an integral part of the practices that we do, since it would be difficult to perturb you as much in a seminar, as it would with a partner. Any kind of agitation, be it by a spouse or by watching violence, become an excellent training ground for learning how to "bypass" the mind.*

One of the most significant practices that I give to my students, is to start resolving conflicts differently than they did before. And personal relationships present the perfect arena for these practices, as is watching violence on TV. Viewing vicious scenes on the screen creates the opportunity to resolve these borrowed conflicts within ourselves and benefit from them, without having to actually go through these difficult experiences in our own lives. These practices really speed up the integration phase considerably.

And by the way, "bypassing" the mind is the key to resolving all the problems in the world, which at this point is highly needed if we are to survive in it.

> It would be difficult to perturb you as much in a seminar, as it would be with a partner.

Believe it or Not... Meditation Can be An Obstacle

Zoltan: So, what are some of the things that you consider to be obstacles on the path to awakening?

> The ability to resolve conflicts differently is one of the immediate benefits of awakening on a personal level as well as on a global scale.

Gabor: The prime and perhaps the only obstacle is not understanding that the approach to awakening, up until now, has been faulty. The whole approach must be different. The bundle that contains the same value system, belief system and cumulative system that we hold so dear and that we hope will deliver us from the chaos and confusion of this 3rd dimension, is the biggest obstacle.

> Expecting to be awakened using the value system of our contrast-reality, is the same as expecting to satisfy our hunger by taping sandwiches on our body.

Knowing how the mind currently works, various Sirens parading as spiritual concepts, are packaged and made very attractive - not unlike any product that we would buy on the TV shopping channel or in a fancy store in a shopping mall. They exude the charm and appeal that seduces us and makes us feel that we really, really "need" them. The "spiritual shopping center" is huge and it has an infinite number of shopping seekers who are continuously dazzled by the shiny objects of delusion and who bask in the mental bliss of comparing – not only prices, but all sorts of beliefs, values, theories, templates and even mysteries.

Zoltan: *So, do you mean to say that there is no value to meditation or other spiritual practices?*

Gabor: *There is plenty of value to all these for relaxation and having a better life filled with good temporary feeling and meaning. However, they sedate you into a blissful and relaxed state of "mind", which is neither conducive to awakening, nor does it provide the motivation necessary to leap into the unknown. Contrary to common spiritual beliefs, "feeling good" is not necessarily the optimal condition for awakening. It is actually much easier to enter the "Golden Ratio Gate" using the physiology of a "sad mode".*

In the common linear type of meditation, "feeling good" is the opposite of "feeling bad". The normal human mind would assume that "feeling good" must be very close to the feeling of awakening. The spiritual unquestioned assumption: "Surely the increase of feeling good by meditating must be bringing me closer to the gate of heaven" is rampant among seekers who are still in the mind. From the mind's perspective this makes total sense, not realizing that awakening is "non-sensical". It is NON-SENSE!

Meditation as we know it, and similar practices, encourage continuity and the frame-of-mind: "the more the better and, therefore, we will get there." Accumulating and practicing a wonderful mental attitude, where continuity is reinforced – not the interruption – keeps you in the spiritual

> **Contrary to common spiritual beliefs, "feeling good" is not the optimal condition for awakening. It is actually much easier to enter the "Golden Ratio Gate" using the physiology of a "sad mode".**

"smart wheels" of the "Aha Gates". To be present we require the practice of interruption. It is imperative to STOP the habit of thought stream continuation – spiritual or otherwise – to get out of the 3rd dimension clutches of the existing templates. This is a very important point. Once you get this, the doors of simplicity will keep on opening for you.

__Zoltan:__ Why can't I have both – the good feeling and the awakening?

__Gabor:__ You can certainly have both. And, by the way, the "good feeling" that awakening brings is a much better "good feeling" than the one produced by the positive end of the mind's swing. Wanting to retain the positive end of this swing, while enjoying BEING, would be like going to a first-class buffet and searching for the spam.

Awakening is the ability to "bypass" the mind's participation when necessary. There are rules and preferences to most meditations, such as: sit upright with a straight back, close your eyes, look up, place your tongue in a certain position, repeat a specific mantra, meditate twice a day, best time is in the early morning, etc. etc. This is perfectly fine if you want to have a template in your mind, called "meditation" in which your neurons fire together to formulate a new neuro-net connection. This will secure the mind's participation via this template and will always bring the past forward, assuring that you will not be in the present moment, as your mind will continue to thrive on comparing one meditation session with another and judging your success.

Awakening is the ability to "bypass" the mind's participation
moment to moment.

FIRING UP FOR TAKE-OFF!

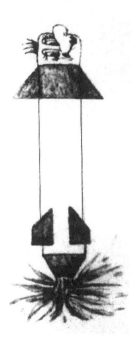

ARE WE THERE YET???

CONTEXTUAL SHIFT AT THE "GOLDEN RATIO GATE"

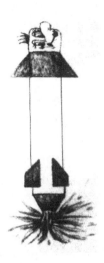

Is Your Load Too Heavy?

It is quite evident that resolving our problems with our current consciousness and competencies is becoming more and more difficult. This is one of the reasons that awakening is happening now with such intensity.

Question by Albert Muller: Should I not get my life in order before I embark on this awakening path? I just lost my job, I have a huge mortgage and my wife is now really pissed off at me. Should I not fix those things first?

Gabor: Yes, absolutely, you should proceed to get your life in order. What I have a problem with, is the word "before" – as in fixing your life before you embark on the path of awakening. You should do it "in conjunction" with your awakening practice. Not before! It is exactly the lack of the "unifying skill" that contributed to your situation. One of the fringe benefits of awakening is that it offers resolutions to problems from a much higher platform.

Humanity has lost a great deal of the powers it once had and humans are missing essential abilities that have become dormant. Awakening practice brings these abilities and powers back to life and as they become available to us, we gain the facility to resolve life's issues in a whole different and lasting way. It is quite evident that resolving our problems with our current consciousness and competencies is becoming more and more difficult. This is one of the reasons that awakening is happening now with such intensity.

Imagine that you have a huge backpack full of rocks, which represent your problems. And unfortunately, more and more rocks are being added daily, until you can hardly walk.

Albert: Yes, that sounds just like my life!

Gabor: Well, what if you had the opportunity to walk into salt water, like the ocean?! Wouldn't those rocks in the backpack instantly feel lighter and easier to handle, as you walk into the water? You would no longer need to struggle with them would you? In the same way, if you shift to an elevated platform, would it not stand to reason that your struggle with life's difficulties would be greatly reduced, as you gain assistance from the universe?

Most people are unaware of this, and therefore they are stuck without universal help. Wouldn't you rather leverage the solution instead of your problems? Expecting to solve your problems before awakening is like expecting a toothless tiger to chew its meat without its dentures.

The Never-Ending Insanity

In a previous chapter I used the triangle to demonstrate how we attempt to resolve our problems in this contrast-reality, through crisis, critical mass and usually, a destructive solution. This was shown in diagrams 4 and 5, which are here below for you to review.

Personal level

Violent Solution
End the Marriage (divorce)

Critical mass	**Crisis**
Can't Stand to be Together	**Bad Marriage**

DIAGRAM 4

Global level

**Violent Solution
- War...Kill!!!**

Critical mass   Crisis
People are Starving   Bad Economy...Not Enough Jobs

DIAGRAM 5

In order to have an easier understanding, it is essential to comprehend things in terms of the triangle-tetrahedron relationship.

I also spoke about how (using geometry as a metaphor), in the 4th progression from a triangle, we "progress" to a tetrahedron, which is the birth of a new way of equalizing and problem solving. It is the realm of cosmic order, where unseen forces are in unlimited supply, since we are connected to the universal flow by having entered into the domain of the golden ratio. I promised to explain this in greater depth in this chapter, so here it is.

Let's first take a closer look at the triangle that is representing (for the sake of explanation) the 3rd dimensional contrast-reality. As we zoom into it, we find that inside it, there is a web of small triangles all linked together (see diagram 9 below).

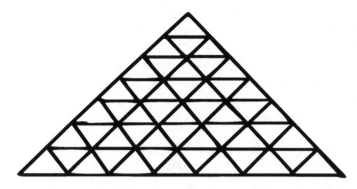

Diagram 9. - The triangle web within the contrast-reality triangle.

The little triangles represent the various aspects of our current life, such as, family, finances, relationships, careers, etc. All these triangles are held together and held in place by triangular structural integrity. When the triangles have proper structural integrity, it means that life is good in this 3rd dimensional world. We are doing well within our family life, our finances are just fine, we have good relationships etc. Just imagine that the corners of each triangle are connected with strings that are pulled with the right tension to its neighbouring corners and to the other triangles, as is shown below, in diagram 10.

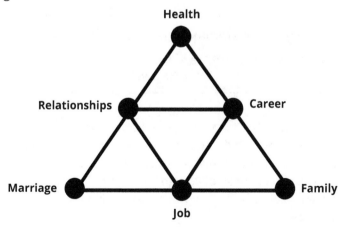

Diagram 10. - Small section of triangle web – all is good in life.

We all know that this is not realistic, since we live in a contrast-reality and something usually happens to throw off our equilibrium. What happens when we lose a job for example? In this case, it would seem as though the string connecting to "Job" or perhaps to "Career" might be cut, leaving the other connecting strings loose and wobbly. In other words, we lose our job and other areas such as career, marriage or even health can suffer. See diagram 11 below.

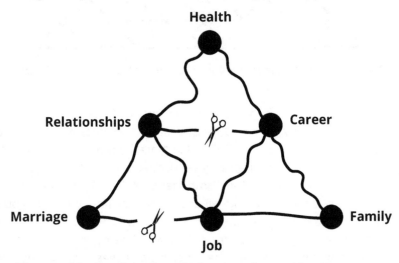

Diagram 11. - Small section of triangle web – problem occurs.

> ## *"Life is one damned thing after another!"*
> **Winston Churchill? Mark Twain? The Easter Bunny?**
> **Who knows!**

Suddenly the structural integrity is compromised and we do whatever we can to "fix" the situation. We might start looking for another job, request a loan from the bank, ask our spouse to work longer hours etc. All these of course, are normal reactions. However, they often result in conflicts in other areas of life and they seldom go away for good.

> We can't fix our way, think our way, spiritualize our way, legislate our way, heal our way, manipulate our way, or emote our way out of contrast-reality.

To continue on the flat path of fixing triangles is not going to work for long. Working on the triangles with the help of the spiritual teachings that emphasize continuity i.e. the Sirens, will also not work... Nor will the accumulation of personal-growth-type knowledge from books and seminars.

Spiralling Out of (limited personal) Control

Earlier in this book I stated that the "Golden Ratio Gate" is the world we need to become "aware" of as an underlying base, that spirals through all existence. It is interwoven like a magic carpet with all living realities. In diagram 12 below, you can see how the spirals of the existential reality weave throughout our triangular flat reality. Obviously, this is just an illustration. The essential point to take away from this is that we ARE connected to the golden ratio reality and at any given moment, we can leap out of our warped triangles - instead of trying to fix them - and step into the ratio reality, the new platform.

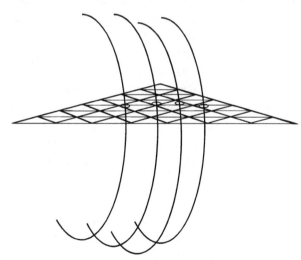

Diagram 12. – Spiral interwoven with Triangle View from Top

Human Transformation - From Content to Context

So how would we leap from this contrasted triangular life to the new platform of living represented by the tetrahedron, where problems are universally resolved with permanent results? For this to occur, a contextual shift is required. To understand this shift, I refer you to the analogy of fruit in a fruit bowl. The bowl is the context, and the fruit is the content.

Life in the triangle reality is like the fruit, and the bowl represents the tetrahedron. To move from a triangular flat existence to the spaciousness of the tetrahedron, we need to understand that it is not the content (the fruit) that has to change, but rather the object that holds them – the bowl, the context. When we replace the bowl with a basket, we have a different context for the fruit. The fruit is the same, but the new context, the basket, changes the space within which the fruit is being held. If we have leaves of lettuce, slices of tomato, pieces of onion and slivers of cucumber spread out on the floor – these are viewed as garbage. If we put them all in a nice bowl, it is salad. How the space is occupied or held is where the transformation happens.

The fruit is just fruit. One piece of fruit may affect another, but not the basket. It is only the context that affects how they are held. In other words, the context affects the content, but not the other way around. I use the bowl and fruit example to explain the relationship between content and context and how it also relates to the relationship between the Sirens and transformation. Just as we are not concerned about the fruit - we don't care whether they originated in ancient Greece and were blessed by a Rabbi - in the same way, it is irrelevant to us if a certain meditation, introduced by a siren, originated in ancient India or in Japan.

The Sirens say "I will give you better quality fruit... they come from Peru. I will give you more exciting meditation with a great ability to astral travel." However, no amount of quality or quantity improvements of the content within the bowl will influence the bowl in any way. In the example of the bowl of fruit, the explanation is on a visual level.

On a mental level, we have the example of a debate, where we use "reframing" of the context to suit our agenda. I can say "Under the previous government, unemployment went up to 10%." This is said in the context of bad news. Now, I can change the context by offering the same information in the context of good news by saying, "Under the previous government, unemployment went up to 10%, which is less than it has been in the past few years." So, the info/content is the same, but in each case, the context is different.

> **Human transformation is a contextual shift on a feeling/ kinesthetic level. Of all living things, only humans are equipped for this kind of contextual feeling shift. This is the factory-built-in skill that needs to be reactivated. When we have our attention in the body, there is a possibility of a "feeling" contextual shift.**

We are already using re-contextualizing in words and in our minds. The mental reframing is a contextual shift, as we are changing the way we look at things without changing the facts. I used to have friends who went to an Ivy League school, where this kind of "reframing" was taught as common practice in the study of debates.

Human transformation is a contextual shift on a feeling or kinesthetic level. A human being is capable of a feeling-related change of context. Of all living things, only humans are equipped for this kind of contextual feeling shift. It comes about by being in the body and feeling space. This is the new skill that we talk about, which needs to be activated. When we have our attention in the body, there is a possibility of a "feeling" contextual shift. This is the factory-built-in interface that we have, and that must be awakened. It is not visual or mental. It is kinesthetic.

The Home of the Permanent Resolutions

So - I go within, I activate this new spatial interface and now, with my new skill, through my new instrument (newly activated feeling body) and I feel space. The ability to feel space is the same thing as being able to change the bowl to a basket at will. This is the shift from the triangular flat life situation to the space of a tetrahedron – a contextual shift. While the senses sense content, the human body - once activated by focusing the attention inside – senses the context. In fact, the activated body not only has the ability to create the context, but it can also regulate it. This is really the whole point of transformation.

At this stage, I still have my templates and all the content of the "Aha Gates". However, I am now capable, at will, of changing the bowl to a basket, or even a to a football field. So, I am not only able to prevent my fall, I can also raise the floor. In this context of spatial/feeling existence, as in the tetrahedron, or in the body, the thought stream and the emotional hurts - that normally feed the "smart wheels" and their templates – can be neutralized and rendered ineffective.

When these are no longer fanning the flames of human problems – i.e. content – the context is the throne and problems can be naturally dissipated. In the Golden Age there were no problems... only harmony, peace and prosperity. People lived in the context of spatial feeling with no thought streams that deviated from the golden ratio. Therefore, humans did not create problems through the mental processes that are rampant today. Returning to this original HOME land, through the "Golden Ratio Gate", releases the charge of all suffering and resolves our made-up problems.

The 4th Progression Significance Summary

Having said all the above, let me remind you that there really is no triangle or tetrahedron. These are just visual representations used to elaborate on the significance of the 4th progression. As I mentioned earlier in this book, the area of "entry" through the "Golden Ratio Gate" – the 4th progression – must be understood and it is also essential to understand the triangle-tetrahedron relationship.

So, I repeat: at this place, that we are calling the 4th progression, there is no longer a linear progression. Here there is no progression, but a "leap". Although from the 4th progression and on, we can enter the "Golden Ratio Gate" or the golden ratio reality, we cannot "continue" into it. We must "leap" out of the contrast-reality into the 4th progression at an angle. This is a point of leaping, angling, surrendering. This is where the mind begins to acquire its angling abilities.

> **The leap out of our contrast-reality triangles is not a forward linear- progression leap. It is an "ANGULAR LEAP".**

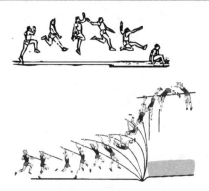

Unlike the "long-jump", leaping out of the contrast-reality must be at an angle, just as a pole vaulter does to get to the "other side".

Understanding the 4th progression helps us greatly, when we are trying to resist the temptation to chase after false spiritual concepts and beliefs (i.e. content), rather than putting our attention where it belongs – **PARTIALLY INSIDE**. This is precisely why we keep explaining it in different ways and from various angles. Once we start to see things in the "context" of the 4th progression, we can have clearer and deeper understanding.

As you can see, context is very important, and so I will now summarize and bring together all the points about the 4th progression.

4th Progression Summary

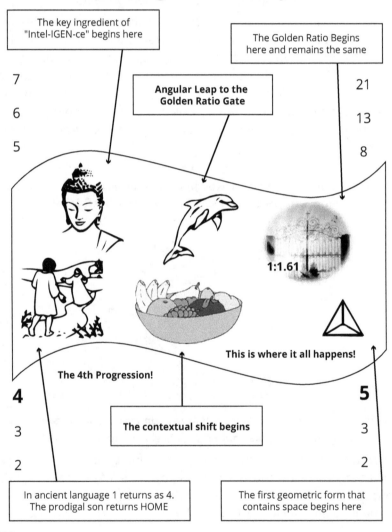

To Bee or Not to Bee

Bees love to fly from flower to flower drinking their nectar. To them, this is what life is about. However, their real purpose is to cross-pollinate those flowers. Without those bees and their cross-pollinating service, we would lose much of our vegetation, and eventually, our lives.

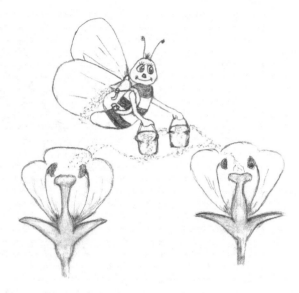

Sometimes, life has a different intention than the one we are able to see. We think that the purpose of our difficulties in life is to make us stronger. Some say, "What doesn't kill you, will make you stronger!" or "Obstacles show up for our personal growth and to burn our karmas." And others say that God must be pissed off. When we are in trouble on a global scale, with famines, wars, and other catastrophes, we ask every spiritual or religious leader within shooting distance "Why is God so mean?".

But in reality, our difficulties are none other than portals to transcend or to wake up from this contrast dimension. Instead of chasing after improvements in an attempt to "fix" our life, we need to see that, just as life has a different intention for the bees, it also has a different intention for us, namely transformation.

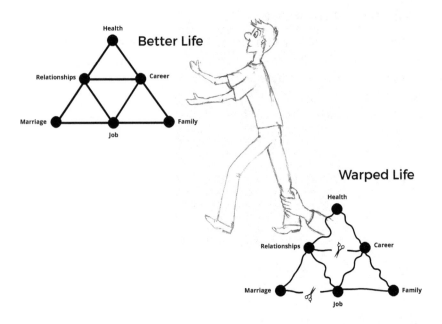

The purpose of this book is precisely to show you how to use these portals to your advantage, if life offers them to you. If life does not give you a difficulty/portal, you can learn how to transcend anyway.

We No Longer Need to Wait for a Tragedy!

Question by Rebecca Scott: I seem to be attracting a lot of hardships and difficulties in my life. Is this because subconsciously I feel that I need some suffering in order to progress in my awakening?

*Gabor: There is no exact answer to that. The fact is that you are having difficulties. There is not much use in analysing whether your difficulties are created by your subconscious or not. It is not important to know why these hardships have been manifested. What is essential, is to adopt an attitude that is most conducive for our awakening. By working with people, I have discovered that embracing a healthy mindset **first**, leads to much quicker results. So, here is an example of such a mindset, that you can adopt yourself:*

"I am greatly blessed to attract many access points for my awakening. I know that from the perspective of the universe, this is quite useful, since the universe is now in the phase of evolving through people who are ready to return home through awakening. So, by having more difficulties, I have more access points or portals for awakening. Thus, I am in alignment with the direction that the universe is headed towards."

Rebecca: *So what you are saying is, it doesn't matter why the difficulties are created, but what matters is the attitude. Is that correct?*

Gabor: *Exactly. What matters is the right approach that will lead to results or in other words, awakening.*

Rebecca: *So it would appear, that to get better results, hardships or tragedies are very useful and should be welcomed. Is that so?*

Gabor: *Yes, it is extremely important to know that hardships and tragedies create easier access points. HOWEVER, it is even more important to remember that access points are available to us anywhere and at anytime... with or without hardships. The whole point of this teaching is to know this, and to learn how to create our own access points in the* **absence of difficulties***.*

Rebecca: *Can you elaborate on that?*

Gabor: *Let's say for a moment, that you currently have difficulties. In conjunction with solving and attending to your problems, you will learn how to use them as access points. What you will find, is that the troubles will make it easier to access the ratio-reality and in turn, the ratio-reality will be of great help in resolving your problems. So, you and your difficulties will have a co-catalyst relationship.*

Rebecca: *What if I don't have difficulties?*

Gabor: *Difficulties or not, we have the technology to match the physiology of an easy access point. This is very much encouraged, so that we, as society, start to get used to the fact that this benevolent and loving world is accessible and available to us at anytime. It costs nothing and it is our birthright. In time (so to speak), this nurturing world will become our "default platform" and the likelihood of encountering difficulties in our lives will be much reduced.*

Rebecca: *What do you mean by matching the physiology of an easy* *access point?*

Gabor: *In order to have an access point, the structural integrity of our "normal life" needs to be interrupted (as is shown in diagram 11). This can be accomplished in two ways. The first and the most common way is that life or the universe in its graciousness provides plenty of problems to interrupt this structural integrity.*

The second way is to learn how to self-create an interruption. In other words, we can create the effect on the mind and on the body, as a tragedy would, when it brings about a shock and causes us to stop in our tracks. When we go within, and our attention is placed in the feeling of the inner body, this creates an interruption in the thought stream, since no thought can enter this sacred space. This new environment is similar in nature to the physiology that a shock would cause and this is what is learned in my seminars.

So in conclusion, problems are useful for awakening, since they interrupt the precious network of this life in our lunatic asylum. However, we certainly do not have to wait for them to occur. We now have the technology to generate our own interruptions in order to access the higher platform of existence without difficulties. All my teachings revolve around this point and are the "meat & potatoes" of all my seminars and books.

THE RETURN HOME VIA THE "GOLDEN RATIO GATE"

Stop the "Smart Wheel"! I Want to Get Off!

The mind has a very intimate relationship with the senses. Everything that the senses perceive is picked up, interpreted, compared, analysed, stored away or acted on by the mind. When we use the senses to see, hear, smell, etc., we use the same mechanism of doing and not doing (the sensing).

For example, we see with the eyes and if we choose not to see – it is the eyes that are involved in the act of "not seeing". By shutting the eye lids the eyes are in the function of "not seeing". We hear with the ears and when we choose not to hear, we cover our ears. So the ears are now engaged in the "not hearing". In all cases, the seeing or "not seeing" and the hearing or "not hearing" - the same function occurs: the sense sends a message/sensation to the brain. In the seeing or hearing it is a sensation of something that is being perceived, and in the "not seeing" or "not hearing" the message "no sensation" is sent to the brain. This is the same process that goes on with all our senses.

When it comes to the mind's functionality, which is thinking, there is a subconscious assumption that since the mind (in its current state) is so closely related to the senses, it must also operate in the same manner. In other words – the mind thinks, and we have the option of turning it off to "not think", just as we do with the senses. However, this couldn't be further from the truth. One cannot stop thought with thought. It is impossible to think our way out of thinking.

The "smart wheel" thinking cannot just be shut down or turned off in the same way that we close our eyes or cover our ears. Attempting to switch off thinking by using the same mechanism and process as not seeing or not hearing, will never work. Here we have no "reverse" button. We cannot control thinking as we do with the senses. The only way we can stop the thinking, is by "bypassing" the thinking mechanism entirely.

How do we "bypass" the thinking mechanism?
By the re-activation of the body as a transformational organ through awakening.

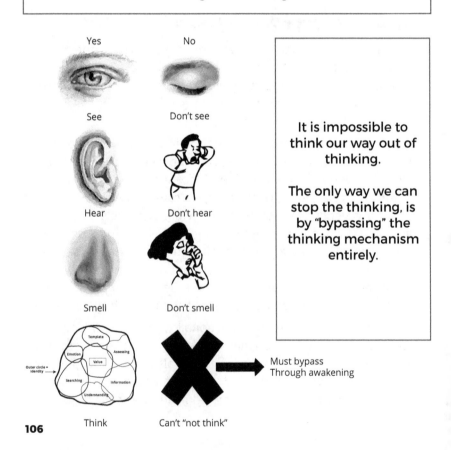

Yes — No

See — Don't see

Hear — Don't hear

Smell — Don't smell

Think — Can't "not think"

It is impossible to think our way out of thinking.

The only way we can stop the thinking, is by "bypassing" the thinking mechanism entirely.

Must bypass
Through awakening

This is the process that is to be engaged in, when attempting to resolve problems in this dimension. In the "Golden Ratio Gate" chapter, I spoke about the normal way in which we resolve our issues in our contrast-reality flat triangles: there is a crisis, we reach critical mass and then, usually, we end up with a destructive resolution. This is due to endeavouring to solve problems with 3rd dimension thinking.

> **Thinking is trying to find solutions to problems that originate in thinking.**
>
> **Positive thinking is still thinking, and it will never elevate one to a new platform.**

When this fails, we try the spiritual way. But as we now know, this is still in the realm of thinking. Positive thinking is still thinking and it will never elevate one to a new platform. Positive thinking cannot be the solution to negative thinking. This is where "bypassing" comes in. When we activate the body as a transformational organ through awakening, the suffering ends, even while the problem is still in existence. In addition, by simply "Being", the problem is usually universally resolved with results that benefit all involved.

Would you ask your goat to guard your cabbage?!

Would you ask your thinking mechanism to guard you against unwanted thinking?!

Turn the Other Cheek

Perhaps the act of "bypassing" that is mentioned above, is what Jesus meant by "Turn the other cheek." In my opinion, this was not an instruction for a behavior modification, but rather a metaphor for turning to a different faculty that I call "bypassing".

The slap on the first cheek represents the problem. Slapping a person back is like continuing to engage in the same mode. Turning the other cheek is turning your attention away from the slapper/problem/thinking and using the "bypassing" technique to elevate one's self to a platform where all is resolved via the intelligence of the universe or the golden ratio reality.

Attention all Thinkers!

Question by Carla Greenspan: *My mind is so busy all the time. I went to plenty of mind control seminars and practiced all kinds of techniques, but I just can't stop my mind. I have heard you speak a lot about the importance of attention. How can I use my attention to stop my mind from running all the time?*

Gabor: *Your attention is your biggest asset. It has been proven by many experiments that when we observe a stream of light, it behaves differently, depending on our observation. When we look with expectation - i.e. with mind involvement - the stream of light becomes a particle. However, when we are not observing with our mind – by either not looking at all, or by observing consciously – the same stream of light is seen as a wave.*

I don't want to get into this type of science too deeply, but it is crucial to "get" that the material world is not independent of us. And so, here lies the most valuable asset that we have – our attention!

> **The material world is not independent of us!**

Between the "smart wheels" pulling at us consistently and demanding our attention, and the influence of language that has been derived from the "smart wheels" in this contrast-reality, there is little hope of getting out of this mess without the proper use of our attention.

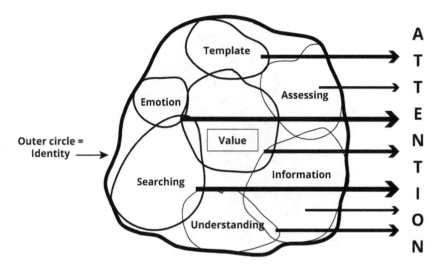

In our unconscious state, we are pulled in so many directions that we don't know any more, if we are coming or going. Our attention chases after any piece of information that matches our familiar templates and we ride that wave for a while. In this state, we become totally oblivious to the fact that, this is a new moment that has nothing whatsoever to do with any of the data that we may have locked into a template created years ago... Using our other interactive mental faculties, such as searching for similar or dissimilar information, comparing, analysing (of course, based on values inherited from a far removed past), and on and on and on...

Needless to say, in a conscious state we would be engaged in "deliberate thinking", in which case the above would not apply. However, in an unconscious state, by the time we are ready to make a coherent assessment or a wise decision, we are totally inebriated with and ensnared by data, concepts, beliefs and theories - much like a drunken spider who gets entangled in its web. This web now becomes a huge Gordian Knot, with no hope of disentanglement.

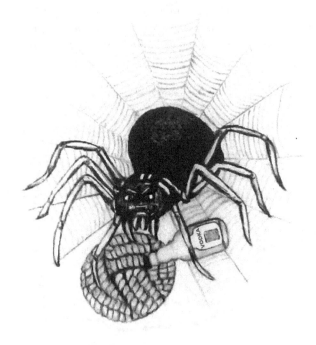

This is where the "Sword of Presence" comes in. Our self-created screwy knot cannot be unravelled. It can only be chopped off by the "Sword of Presence", just as Alexander the Great did with the Gordian Knot in 333 B.C.

In Gordium, by the Temple of Zeus Basilica, was the ox cart that had been put there by the King of Phrygia over 100 years before. The staves of the cart were tied together in a complex knot with the ends tucked away. When Alexander the great arrived there at the age of 23 he was undefeated, but without a decisive victory either. He needed an omen to prove to his troops and his enemies that he was capable of conquering the known world. An oracle had declared that any man who could unravel the elaborate knot, was destined to become ruler of all of Asia. Instead of struggling with the knot, Alexander the Great drew his sword and severed it with one powerful stroke.

When one is present, he/she too has the ability to sever the knot of confusion and delusion with one stroke.

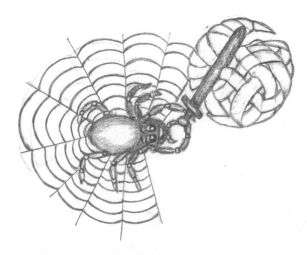

The "Sword of Presence"

Carla: So how exactly does one cut the knot with the "Sword of Presence"?

Gabor: The "Sword of Presence" is an ability that the human mind possesses, but it has yet to be re-activated. This is the process by which we enter into the ratio-based reality from the normal contrast-based reality. The good news is that all the required ingredients to do that are already within us – they are originally "factory-installed".

We first have to learn how to "re-contextualize" the "smart wheel" functions and concepts. In other words, we place them on a different foundation. Remember the bowl with cherries example of "content" and "context"? So here, "re-contextualizing" means that we are changing the bowl. We do this by using the skill of "bypassing".

Once we learn how to "re-contextualize" the contrast mode, the ratio-mode is readily available and not difficult to access. At this stage, consistently measuring, comparing, evaluating, etc., are no longer valued. Thus, it becomes easy to enter the non-dimensional dimension. As soon as we realize that it will not come as a result of alternative facts, again it is relatively easy.

For example, one of my students had a very difficult template called "I am unworthy" to deal with. She had been attempting to get rid of it and *"fix" it for years with the same mind that created it in the first place. She dabbled in hypnotism, repeated powerful affirmations and went to all kinds of therapies and seminars, but without permanent success. At the most she got temporary relief here and there, and then, the same pattern would return.*

In working with her, she learned the skill of "bypassing". Once she was able to "bypass" this template through practice and guidance, she was able to be present with this template - not do away with it or ignore it, but be present with it. At this point her problem was put on a new foundation. It was as if she would say to it, "I see you from my elevated platform as a welcomed guest and yet, a 'no-longer-needed' template. In this new context, I can BE with you without pain or emotion and free you." As she continued with her practice, eventually (for lack of better word) this template, which was no longer receiving the habitual "smart wheel" re-enforcement, was de-throned and neutralized, leaving her free and confident in her own skin again.

What Are the "Factory-Installed" Ingredients?

Carla: *So, what are the "factory-installed" ingredients required for this?*

Gabor: *The two main ingredients needed to accomplish this are: the human body, which I can see that you have, and your ability to pay attention. The attention must be totally freed up from all the attention-getters of the contrast-reality. This is what I call "liberated attention". Once your attention is freed up by your free will, the "liberated attention" is placed within the body itself. Now your most precious asset, the attention, is helping you to line up with the already existing intelligence of the body. With our limited contrast-base mind we couldn't run our body for one second.*

Why not capitalize on our most precious asset
– OUR HIGHLY POTENT ATTENTION – by aligning it with the
existing SUPER UNIVERSAL INTELLIGENCE... replicated as
OUR VERY OWN BODY?!

The body literally has millions of pieces of "information-exchanges" running all the time. In the process of awakening (for lack of better word), when we are able to position our attention in the body itself, we can get in touch with the intelligence that runs the body. And as you now know, the body and the intelligence that runs it are in the ratio-based reality. So, once we are aligned with this intelligence, we are on a whole different platform and we become aware of the interwoven-ness of the universe. The moment we are aware of this interwoven-ness, the mind is automatically "bypassed", as it loses its hold on us in this realm.

Operating from this new platform (new to us... but it has been there all along) is what we can call the "Sword of Presence". At the same moment when our body is activated, which we call the "Sword of Presence", we are already using that "Sword of Presence".

In this game of life, who would you rather have on your side? Your fearful, manipulated, sense-based and limited "pre-activated" mind, riddled with biased and crippled templates? Or the "awakened" mind that is fed and nourished by the supreme intelligence of the universe?

IN-Bodiment – Put All Your Eggs in This Basket!

Carla: What do you mean by placing attention on the body?

Gabor: Not "on" the body, but "IN" the body.

Carla: Oh! Are you referring to embodiment?

Gabor: No. I call it "IN-bodiment", which is not the same as embodiment. Most people use the word embodiment to indicate that a skill is being practiced and imbibed. "IN-bodiment" means to actually sense the inner vitality of the body and live from that platform of existence. It is a skill that is learnt in my seminars and in private sessions, where techniques and practices are taught in order to assist in activating this skill - as well as integrating it in one's life, for the purpose of making it permanent and enabling "Functional Silence" to "regain the throne".

In the meantime, here is a self-qualifying exercise that you can do:

keep your eyes open, and without looking at your hand, feel it. Become completely aware of it. If you are ready for this and willing to try it, notice that your mind will either slow down or even come to a halt.

On the other hand, you might also observe the mind's tendency to dismiss it by saying, "Oh, this is too simple!" or "I already heard this". If the latter occurs, recognize that your mind is still in control through its attempts to compare this to something it heard before and/or to evaluate it, as it does with everything else, even though it cannot comprehend this type of simplicity in its current state. It is only the mind that gets bored with simplicity, and this is because it has not yet learned to value it.

Free Will

Carla: *What do you mean by free will? Some teachers say we don't have free will. So, do we really have it and what is it?*

Gabor: *Free will is the human ability to focus the attention within the body, even though there is absolutely no motivation to do so from the mind and from society as a whole. (I mean "actually" feeling inside and not just talking about it!)*

The concept, or template, called "free will" is not free will. As soon as there is a thought stream attached to what society calls free will, it is no longer free will, because now the thought stream or template has motivational factors built into it. What most people call free will is rather a preference that is predicated upon accumulated templates. For example, if I think I have the free will to choose between a blonde or a brunette and I choose the blonde, it is simply because I have a template that says, "My mother was blonde and a brunette once broke my heart."

There is no freedom in that. It is our templates and past impressions that are choosing on our behalf and giving us reasons to pick this or that with a pre-determined expectation for a desired outcome, or a fear-based resistance to an unwanted outcome. Any damage that we incur in life causes an emotional charge. The emotion then selects a decision that leads to an action, based upon the emotion's damaged value system and most importantly, the degree to which it influences one's identity.

So basically, it is the "damage" that does the choosing, instead of the free will.

*Free will means exercising the choice to go within "**JUST BECAUSE**" ... with no expectation for a desired outcome. Even the thought, "God, I want nothing!" is not nothing. It is a thought or a condition that is the opposite of something. Free will is free even of this thought.*

The Graduation of Free Will

From this point, we are going to graduate the term "free will" and use the term "freed will". It is not the person who is "free" to choose, but rather the will itself becomes "freed" of all thoughts, expectations, ruling templates etc., and is now "free" to choose Home. It must be completely freed to make this choice. Otherwise the fear/desire based narratives will intervene and choose for us and they will never choose anything that is unfamiliar to them.

This is why, unless we have exercised this "freed will" and have become comfortable with it, regardless of the lack of "sense verification and confirmation", the Sirens that dazzle our senses and mind, will almost always have the upper hand.

> **Freed will: "I choose this just because.... (nothing). With no expectation and no concept! I stand naked before thee with pure humility and simplicity... straight from my heart."**

This explains too, why people who have been beaten up by life and are broken down, have an easier time waking up. Individuals who have great tragedies or shocking experiences get short circuited, and their templates are blown. They become humble and lose their fight. They no longer have what it takes to sustain their templates.

At this point, under these unusual circumstances, there is the possibility that their "freed will" may be accessed with greater ease, allowing them to go within with no expectation and just BE. Unfortunately, we also find that at times, a tragedy can be so severe that one may simply give up, rather than use this opportunity for awakening, especially if they are not aware of this option.

> **Reminder: The objective of this work is to awaken without tragedy!**

How Hard is it to BE?

Carla: Ok, so let's say I am willing and I choose to go within and practice this. What's the next step and how hard is it?

Gabor: The initial step of going within is easy, once you have applied your "freed will" and a few techniques with no expectation... and without the pull of the thought streams, generated by your "smart wheels". The next phase involves going deeper within, being able to stay there, activating the transformation body to the fullest, and integrating this new platform in everyday life in a permanent way.

All this is not linear and is not in time but since we only have the dualistic language at our disposal right now, I am compelled to say that there are several practices and steps - that appear to take time - to accomplish the skill of living consistently from the new platform. Each of these steps is reconciled to the moment and this is where a master's help comes into play (and I am talking here about a master who is able to BE... in time and not in time). The detailed instructions are rather individual and specific to each person. They are not standardized. There are no cookie-cutter practices.

This phase is not hard at all. The "duality-language-dominated-mind" labels things easy or hard, depending on whether it can control or understand what is happening. Yes, the integration takes time in the linear-time framework. **HOWEVER***, it is only hard from the mind's perspective, since the mind – as smart as it is – cannot do anything with it. So, to answer your question, it is not at all hard.*

How hard could it be to be as you truly are?

Why would the creator make it hard for us to go HOME?

The only difficulty is when we attempt to wake up by using the same habitual approach that worked for us in the "Aha Gates", that the New Age industry is enticing us with. When we do this, it is still not difficult... it is IMPOSSIBLE! This is why I usually say that awakening or IN-bodiment is either easy or impossible, depending on how much baggage you are attempting to bring in, when you try to enter the "eye of the needle".

> Awakening is either easy or IMPOSSIBLE!

How Often Should We "BE NOW"?

Carla: And the practices that you give, how often should they be done? If I want this to be a permanent experience, does that mean I have to practice all the time?

Gabor: Not all the time... just NOW... and NOW... and NOW... ha ha.... I am not trying to make light of this. It is best to practice as many times a day as you can, but be easy about it. Don't be too serious about it. It works much better with a light heart, and occasionally, I recommend adding laughter. There are no specific times to practice.

This is not like the divisive approach of linear meditation, where you pick a certain time to be holy and peaceful, while the rest of the day you are back to being the same unconscious being, dragged around by a duality-based mind. Or, where you have to sit in a certain way at a specific spot, with incense and candles and all kinds of rules and restrictions.

Going within has no rules and limitations. It is not a separate event in your day. Practicing presence is done in every moment that you are aware of it. All life situations and experiences become your training ground, where you have an opportunity to re-proportion your attention – i.e. focusing most of your attention within the body, while retaining some of it outside - and act in the world from your inner space as a conscious being.

> All life situations and experiences become your training ground, where you have an opportunity to re-proportion your attention.

How many times a day you practice, or how long you stay within – these are individual and custom made programs. With practice, it will eventually, (for lack of better word) become your new default place to return to with great ease. At first the magnetic pull of the "smart wheels" is very strong and it will do everything in its power to get you back to its "Aha Gates" and habitual thinking. The mind will fight to regain its control. But as you continue to "bypass" it and go within, using the practices assigned to you, the magnetic pull will loosen up and it will stop imposing on you, and your "will" will be freed to BE HOME.

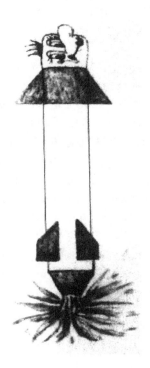

The "Freed will" ignites and initiates the take-off!

THE FINAL
NEVER-ENDING FRONTIER

FROM "PORTAL" TO
"FREEDOM" AND BEYOND

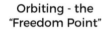
Orbiting - the
"Freedom Point"

Leaving earth's magnetic field
through IN-bodiment.

The "lift-off" ignited by free will.

THE INTEGRATION CURVE

The Inter-woven-ness of the "Golden Ratio Gate" Spiral

Although the "Aha Gates" and the "Golden Ratio Gate" are so completely different, as I have shown in diagram 8 (see below), the "Golden Ratio Gate" spiral runs through the "Aha Gates", allowing us access to it at any moment throughout our lives. For this reason, the inter-woven-ness of the spiral is very important to understand.

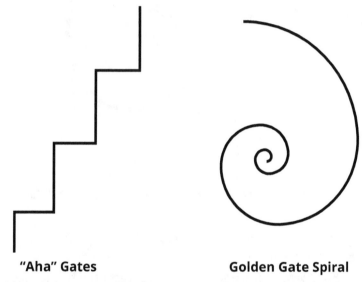

"Aha" Gates   Golden Gate Spiral

Diagram 8. – "Aha Gates" & "Golden Ratio Gate" Spiral Comparison

Even though the contrast-reality and the ratio-reality are interwoven, we study them and illustrate them separately for easier understanding. Diagram 13 below shows how the "Golden Ratio Gate" spiral is interwoven with the "Aha Gates". I will be using this diagram to demonstrate the "Integration Curve" that begins at the moment of awakening.

The curve that you see is just a segment. It really goes on and on, as we continue to integrate our new platform with life in this dimension. When you look at this diagram, just imagine that the curve or the spiral is lifting out from the page, since it is not flat. It is a leap-off point at an angle, which is addressed in more depth in the advanced seminars.

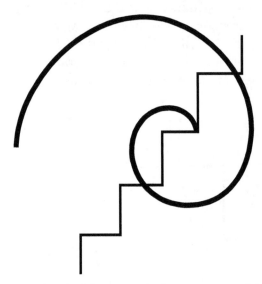

Diagram 13. – "Golden Ratio Gate" Spiral Interwoven with "Aha Gates"

As you can see, in diagram 14 below, the "Integration Curve" has several significant points:

a. The ***"Portal"*** - the point of entry, represented by the black dot at the beginning of the curve. This is where the "angular" leap from the contrast-reality to the Ratio-reality takes place.

b. The ***"Honeymoon Curve"*** – a short segment that begins at the "portal".

c. The ***"Judas Curve"*** - a longer segment, illustrated by the dotted line, that starts at the "portal" and ends at the "Freedom Point".

d. The ***"Freedom Point"*** – indicated by a small line at the end of the "Judas Curve".

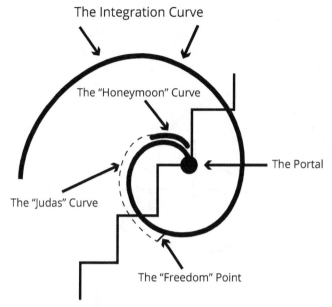

Diagram 14. – The "Integration Curve"

The "Portal" - "Life-Created"

The "portal" is the access point where one has the opportunity to leap from the "Aha Gates" and enter the "Golden Ratio Gate" spiral. This is the same "portal" mentioned at the end of the previous chapter, that we can use to transcend or to wake up, from this contrast dimension, as is show in diagram 15 below. The warped triangle on the bottom if you remember, represents the difficult life situation when the structural integrity of our "ideal" life has been broken. This creates what I call the "Life-Created Portal".

This is the "portal" that we access when life gives us a shock and creates an interruption, such as losing our job, falling ill, etc. Often this can be painful or even tragic. Many people either fall into self-pity or misery at this point or - if they are the fighting type who have strong "self-improvement" templates – they may struggle to overcome their problem, once the shock wears down.

However, one who has learned how to use the "shock & bypass" technology, has the opportunity here to leap out of the contrast-reality, before the mind quickly jumps in to repair the problem. What is needed here is the use of one's "freed will" and the skill to maintain the "portal" and move along the curve to real freedom.

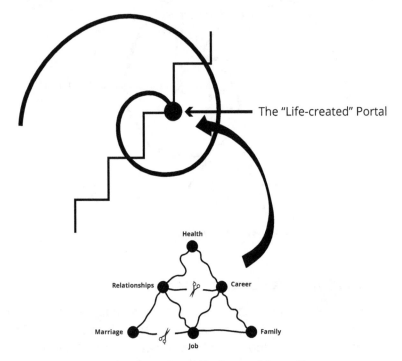

Diagram 15. – "Life-Created Portal"

The "Portal" - "Self-Created"

As was mentioned in a previous chapter, we don't need to wait for a tragedy or a catastrophe to shock us into the "portal". Besides the "Life-Created Portal" there is also what I call the "Self-Created Portal" which we can create when life is good, as is shown in diagram 16. This "portal" is created by using our "freed will" and by combining the "interruption" and the "bypassing" techniques that are taught in my seminars.

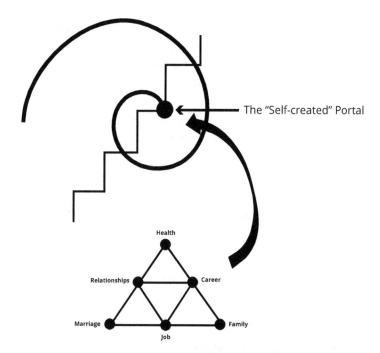

Diagram 16. – The "Self-Created Portal"

What Are the Road-blocking Barricades at the "Portal"?

Entering the "portal" could be the easiest thing to do if it weren't for its two main mind-based, road-blocking barricades:

a. Its "breaking-new-ground", rare, unthinkable and borderline perturbing simplicity. In fact, it is the extreme simplicity itself that at times, makes one miss it altogether... like riding in a fast train through a tiny village – if you blink, you miss it.

b. The onslaughts of a whole lot of "smart wheels" that will stop at nothing in their attempts to invalidate any intention to even try it.

"There is another way of doing it. I just want to keep doing what I am doing, and I will get there eventually." This is what we often hear from people who will, most likely, never make an attempt to go within. Usually, people who are entrenched in their own "continuity-type" spirituality, fall into this category. They are convinced that awakening can only be gotten as a result of continuation. We now know that this is not so. It is in the interruption, in the abrupt stopping, that awakening becomes a possibility.

Other common thoughts of resistance are, "I am finding a wide range of exciting opportunities and choices in what I am currently doing, so I am going to stay with that." This usually comes from seekers who have just started their search and are enthusiastic about the outer trimmings.

And then there are the famous opposite mind sets:

a.   "I already heard all about this. Yeah, yeah…. I know." And its counterpart…

b.   "How come I have never heard about this? Can't be real if I haven't heard about it."

Mirror, Mirror on the Wall…

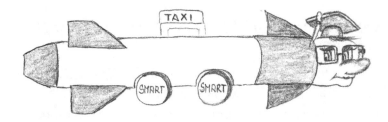

Which is the Deadliest Road-blocker of Them All?

In the entire "Integration Curve", and even before the entry, there is a standard poisonous statement or question:

"It's the same as…" or "Isn't it just like…?"

It is an innocent looking poisonous snake, mascaring as a smart owl. It is utilizing the comparing/analysing function, that is very useful and desirable in the "smart wheels" of contrast-reality. However, in the context of awakening, it puts it in the realm of content. It instantly changes a context into content, achieving the opposite results of the contextual shift that is required for awakening.

There is a huge difference between understanding something and "getting it". In understanding, we compare information to an existing template that we have on the same subject. Anything to do with templates of any kind leads to understanding, and this is where "It's the same as..." or "It's like..." are very advantageous.

However, "getting" something is Being... without the engagement of a template in any way. Here the mind-set is:

"I am sitting in it... sitting in the truth. I am not encouraged in any way to engage any one of my templates, or any aspect of my mind. I am not only comfortable, but I am confident that this is for 'real!' No proof is needed." At this stage, "It's the same as..." does not come up. If this is implied in any phase prior to awakening, it becomes a deadly poison that affects the entire process.

The phrase: "It's the same as..." or "Isn't it just like...?" is useful and wise in the contrast-reality. However, if applied in the context of awakening, this innocent looking phrase is a poisonous snake masquerading as a wise owl.

People's opinions encourage this poisonous supposition since there is little to no support, when it comes to awakening. If you have encountered such a conversation and feel overwhelmed by the effects of this covert or overt invalidation – DON'T WORRY! The technology to get you back on track quickly and effortlessly is available.

If you have the need to be popular and get approval, usually the obstacles become insurmountable, so stay low and stop talking for a while. The majority – the masses – are easily manipulated. They are fearful and they viciously guard their identity. Historically, they never go in the "right direction". They are in the "after-effect" of the manipulative forces. So, ask for opinions at your own peril.

I tell my students to notice how a conversation affects them. If it takes them away from presence and throws them into mental content - which is frequently such a strong trap - it is pretty much the time to say good-bye and end that conversation.

The masses are easily manipulated. They are fearful and they viciously guard their identity. They are in the "after-effect" of the manipulative forces.

Entering the "Portal" – With Your Private Key

Mind-based road-blocking barricades aside... when employing our "freed will" (see *"Forget-me-not Definitions" chapter*), there is an attitude or an approach that is required for a smooth and "successful" entry through the "portal", the "eye of the needle". Here is where the ancient language of Magyar comes in handy, giving us words that would otherwise take a few paragraphs to describe the same thing in English. Had the word "secret" not been so overused, I would say the following Magyar word is like a secret code that opens the door of the "portal".

This Magyar word is **Rostokol** (pronounced 'rosh-tok-ol'). It is rarely used in daily conversation. However, it is understood as "I'm sort of hanging out." In decoding this word from presence, it denotes "ancient body-ing" - as if the body itself were a verb. In this context "ancient body" refers to the original creation, when it was known and experienced, that the body of man was a replica of the universe, since it is made in the image and likeness of the same ratio (the golden ratio) that the creator employs to create everything. In other words: the action to take in the direction of the 'ancient body'... without any expectation. So, the translation would be "I'm just sort of sitting... BEING here...being IN the original body... without any anticipation or expectation."

I am using this word here to point to the action/non-action of placing the attention in the body (=universe) with the "just because/ no reason other than BEING" attitude and remaining there with no expectation, with simplicity and humility. **This is the word that calls for the action necessary to open the door.** The next Magyar word that I will share with you, is the result of this action.

Roskad (pronounded 'rosh-kad') literally means "to collapse under a heavy load". When decoded from presence, it indicates that something is collapsing under a heavy load, and because it is ancient (of the original ratio-based nature), it is collapsing under the golden ratio. In other words "I am naturally collapsing... surrendering... converging or merging back into the ancient body (recognized as the ratio-based body) of God... not in a linear mode, but in the coded way that is in keeping with the golden ratio."

While **Rostokol** is the action, the doing/non-doing, **Roskad** is what happens as a result of the surrendered action of the **Rostokol**. (Notice that it took three paragraphs to offer the decoded translation of those two Magyar words.)

The "Honeymoon Curve"

The "Honeymoon Curve" is usually a short period right after the entry. It is different for each person in duration and experience. For the most part, it is a phase in which one is amazed and often excited about the new-found peace and silence. For many it is the first time they have ever witnessed the "stoppage" of their fast-moving mind.

Others, especially those who have been on a spiritual path for many years, are astonished to find that this is very different from regular meditation and many other experiences. There is an indescribable quality to this silence that is unlike anything that belongs to the spiritual world that springs from the "Aha Gates".

It is a wonderful segment of discovery and the practices are engaged with full fervour and curiosity. The only cautionary note for this period is that in one's excitement about the new experience, and not having had enough practice in observing the shenanigans of the mind, there can easily be a tendency to create a new template.

> Those who have been on a spiritual path for many years are astonished to find that entering the "portal" of awakening is nothing like meditation. There is a quality/non-quality to this silence that is unlike anything that belongs to the spiritual world that springs from the "Aha Gates".

As soon as there is a template, comparisons begin to occur. For some people, presence initially may have a "low-key" (*seemingly only!*) feel to it, whereas previous experiences may have appeared to be more intense in comparison to this new reality. This is where doubts may arise and therefore, this is also where an awakened master can help in guarding the newly awakened from the return of the jealous and control-loving mind.

The Undeniable Inner Silence

Question by Linda Jones: *What was the honeymoon phase like for you?*

Gabor: *Having been through such an intense existential crisis, the ability to suddenly go within with ease was amazing! Getting such a sense of peace and relief from depression was a huge and wonderful contrast. So, my "Honeymoon Curve" was accompanied by a warm and fuzzy feeling, much like falling in love. The inner silence was undeniable. No one could tell me that this was not it. I truly "got" that the Kingdom of God is, in fact, within – not as a conceptual understanding, but as a reality. It was a celebratory feeling of Aaaaa... at last I am* **HOME**. *From the mind's perspective, it was somewhat of a shock and I was filled with surprise at how simple and obvious it was, once there was no mental interference in the form of attempting to describe or analyse it.*

It so happened that right around the time of my "honeymoon", a friend of mine sent me a few VHS videos of Eckhart Tolle's lectures. This took me by surprise, since this friend had no money and these tapes were expensive... yet he felt compelled to send them to me without being asked. Well, I did not feel the need to have a teacher at that point, but out of sheer curiosity and respect for my friend, I decided to watch a bit.

I randomly picked up one of the tapes, in no particular order and, lo and behold, the first thing I heard this dear loving man say was, "Look at me, feel your hand and your mind will stop." So, although it didn't seem essential, I was delighted to receive this confirmation and validation of my experience and of the simplicity of this practice.

My mind was now engaged in a very weak and subtle commentary with minor thoughts, such as "I can't possibly share this experience." Or, "I know what I found, but it can't be explained." Or, "I could be quite alone in this." Or, "How will I function and finish my construction project?" etc. These thoughts were also accompanied by the, "I really don't care" kind of attitude. They did not last long as they had no real meaning or value in the realm of Silence, where I was becoming more and more established as my new Abode.

I also realized that all my previous mystical experiences – from kundalini awakenings and visions, to swimming like a dolphin – as wonderful as they felt at the time – were not in the same realm as this peace, which cannot be compared to anything. They were not awakenings. They were merely mystical experiences that are nice to have along the way, but certainly, they are no more essential contributors to awakening than a good dessert or a wonderful orgasm.

HOUSTON, WE HAVE A PROBLEM

The "Judas Curve" – The Danger of Self-betrayal

The "Judas Curve" begins at the "portal", just like the "Honeymoon Curve", only it continues along the spiral until the "Freedom Point". Again, the duration and experience of this curve is not the same for everyone. I call it the "Judas Curve" since this is the segment where one is still pulled by the magnetic field of templates and the "smart wheel" propensities of the "Aha Gates" which can cause a person to fall prey to any of the contrast-reality's tempting distractions. This is where one might betray one's self and give up on awakening, justifying this with all kinds of brilliant and "sensible" excuses and pretexts. The Sirens have a field day with this.

During the "Honeymoon Curve" this is not so noticeable, but once this phase is over, all kinds of habitual and resistant thought streams start to surface. The mind does not want to give up its control and everything it has accomplished over the years prior to awakening, which it still values. It wants to continue being busy and being acknowledged for its continuous efforts. Although it says that it wants the answers to life's existential questions and to find liberation, it is still very much addicted to the search, which it is reluctant to give up.

It fears being left out, and so like Judas, it whispers all sorts of "smart" things in your mental ears to steer you away from presence.

At this stage, you are either conscious or not. When you are conscious i.e. your attention is pulled in, as in IN-bodiment, the "Judas Whispers" are turned off, and you are on track with your integration. When you are not practicing presence/bypassing, and allowing the thought streams to take your attention, you become subject to the attacks of the mind and the "Judas whispers".

This is the time to be very vigilant in exercising ones "freed will". At this phase, the more one practices the "Rostokol" – humbly turning the attention within the body with no expectation - the less force the magnetic pull has, and one's values start to shift in the direction of BEING HOME, while the mind takes a back seat as servant. This is where the "Freedom Point" begins, since the resistance no longer has a hold on the awakened.

Some of the habitual, resistant thought streams that emerge as the mind attempts to take back its control, can be seen in the following examples of common question-like doubts that the self-betraying Judas tends to whisper in seekers' ears, to steer them away from presence.

Common "Judas Whisper" – The Mañana Syndrome

Question by David Golan: I have tried this path and feel good about it, but I just can't find the time to practice. I am a single father with three children and my life is just running around trying to cope. Perhaps this is not the right time for me and I should wait till my kids are older.

Gabor: Oh, yes...this is a very common comment that I hear these days. I call it the Mañana (pronounced manyana) syndrome. Mañana in Spanish means tomorrow. When I lived in Mexico, I noticed that this word was used not as "tomorrow", but rather as "not now". It is a "later" that never comes.

The limited fearful mind, which has not yet acquired the super contextualizing ability, thinks in terms of fear, lack and content. There is always something to be scared of: "never enough money", "never enough time", "how can I get more of...", "how can I protect myself from losing..." etc. Again, the mind thinks in terms of separation and it prioritizes according to its limited values of scarcity. Imagine if the man with the rocks in his backpack, instead of saying, "Where's the beach?" would say, "I don't have time to learn how to walk into the salt water!"

David: But don't I have to set aside some time to do the practice? Like an hour in the morning, or something like that? It would be very difficult for me to find that kind of time these days.

Gabor: Setting aside time for the practice would put the practice in the category of content – a separate event in time. This is the danger of meditation "sessions". In the context of your day (the bowl), the activities are the content (the fruit in the bowl). Your day is filled with all kinds of content – making breakfast, taking the kids to school, going to work... and now you think you have to add another piece of content called, "sitting for an hour and practicing presence". Of course, you won't find time for that. Your day is overflowing with content.

But that is not the kind of practice that we do. We are not interested in turning our practice into a content. Awakening practice is all about contextualization (see previous chapter) which you can only do now, in this moment or in any other moment, no matter what else you are doing. You cannot do your context practice as content. When you are present and functioning from that context of presence, your practice is in context, not content. If you do allow the practice to be content in your timed routine, it will also become a continuation of yesterday's allocated timed practice.

So no, absolutely do not allocate an hour or any time for a practice that can only be practiced now. This practice will lead you "beyond time". You may use all of your life situations for the purpose of practice, as long as the practice is done now – in the moment. You can practice it in the moment that you are working, talking, driving, listening, cooking etc. This way your whole day will be your practice and you will be doing your activities consciously, and within the context of presence.

Please Note:
This is a lot easier that it seems! This is what the training is for!

Common "Judas Whisper" – "I Need to Work on Myself First"

Question by Ann McNiel: *I don't feel I am suitable for this path. I am too impatient, judgemental and resistant. Don't you think I should take some time to work on myself and on my forgiveness, judgement, and other bad habits?*

Gabor: *The erroneous assumption here is that awakening happens at the end of some road, after which we accumulate enough good spiritual behavior and "brownie-points". We think this is going to prepare us for something... for some spiritual reward. It is not an unsmart supposition, since everything we have accomplished in the world came as a result of amassing, improving, gathering more information and "bettering" ourselves, as is normally done in the "smart wheel" reality. For awakening, this is an error, because it is precisely the abrupt and bold stopping of any kind of perpetuation or accumulation that leads there.*

Awakening cannot be achieved as a goal in time. It cannot be reached as a result of behavior modification. Awakening is in the realm of context, not content. Like with the fruit bowl, most studies are about acquiring more and better quality fruit. Using this example metaphorically, the awakening study is the study of the bowl, not the fruit. We can put the fruit in a basket, put it in the middle of a room or put it in a football field. In either case, nothing happens to the fruit.

With the newly awakened human ability, we are able to shift the context and make any number of modifications to it. Working on yourself and cultivating different behaviors would be very much like changing the quality of the fruit in the bowl, and that is not what we are after.

Awakening cannot be achieved as a goal in time.

It is not a behavior modification.

The Mirage on the Other Side of the Fence

Ann: Aren't all the enlightened beings portraying these wonderful behaviors for us as an example of how to be?

Gabor: On the other side of the fence, which is the golden ratio reality, there is only one behavior. It has no name, but for now, we call it presence. **Looking at it from the contrast-reality perspective, the person who is present looks like the opposite of any personal trait that we want to modify.** *If we are addressing any*

> When one is in the "present moment", it only looks like he/she is forgiving, allowing, etc., since ratio-reality is unifying. In the unified reality, there are no such distinctions.

kind of negative behavior like judgment, impatience etc., an awakened person who is present, appears to be the opposite of that – accepting, patient etc. This may motivate us to cultivate forgiveness and patience. This would put us right into "mind-practice". It is an error to say that that person is allowing, accepting, forgiving etc., because this assumption only exists in the contrast-reality mind. For this reason, I call this assumption "The Mirage on the Other Side of the Fence".

In the elevated platform those qualities don't apply. When one is "fully awake" it only looks like he/she is forgiving, allowing etc., since ratio-reality is unifying. In the unified reality, there are no such distinctions. It is only the limited mind that would motivate one to cultivate certain behaviours since it lives in contrast-reality and consistently seeks improvement on its own level.

*When I was sitting with the Indians in Ecuador, my perception of them was that they were accepting me, they were loving me unconditionally, they were patient with me and understanding. However, looking back, I now know that they were simply **BEING**. It was only my mirage of looking at them (the other side of the fence) that caused me to assume all those wonderful qualities about them.*

The Mirage on the Other Side of the Fence!

Common "Judas Whisper" – "I Need to Heel my Emotions"

Ann: What about releasing negative and painful emotions? Don't I have to let go of them somehow first?

Gabor: No. For several reasons: The first being, just what we discussed. It is counter-productive to engage in "gathering" or "getting rid of" emotions or feelings on the path of awakening. Collecting more or dissolving more – both of these are in the realm of accumulation and amassing more content, which is the biggest hindrance to awakening. By getting rid of emotions we assume that we are acquiring "extra purity" and "lightness of spirit". Hence, the supposition that eventually we will get to our lofty destination.

Secondly, by ridding ourselves of difficult emotions, we could be depriving ourselves of an easier way to leap out of the contrast-reality. We may be missing out on an easier way to access the "portal" that would catapult us into the elevated platform of the ratio-reality.

Recently, a friend on Facebook initiated a discussion on the topic of "letting go", to allow friends to express the various areas where they felt they needed to release something that was standing in their way of awakening. For this purpose, he posted the following fill-in-the-blank statement: "Letting go of_____."

Within two days, there were 73 comments from people who filled the blank with all kinds of emotions. Among these were: fear, resistance, doubt, negativity, attachments, constraints, sadness, selfishness, and on and on. It is fine to say we need to let go of these issues. The biggest problem though, is that by saying this, we are also triggering the opposite – letting go and not letting go. So in effect, we are reinforcing our position in the duality swing, which in the long run, does not get rid of anything.

Ann: So what should I do then, when I am trying to practice being present, and some strong emotions suddenly erupt and want to take over?

Gabor: Be with it. Be with the emotion. By Being with something – whether it be fear, doubt, or any other emotion, the so-called "letting go" will happen of it own accord, and this will be permanent. We are not *saying not to deal with emotions or difficulties. We are saying – you are better off dealing with them in conjunction with presence practice. And, by the way, you will be amazed with your results.*

> By dealing with difficult emotions separately from presence practice (namely, the "bypassing" method), we may be missing out on an easier way to access the "portal" that would catapult us into the elevated platform of ratio-reality.

Common "Judas Whisper" – Sunday Church Mentality

Question by Mario Pellegrin: I like your work and sometimes it feels good and sometimes I don't feel anything. To be honest with you, I don't practice regularly... just once in a while when I remember.

Gabor: This is what I call the "Sunday Church Mentality", where you kind of go there and kind of practice once in a while... just as you go to church, out of a feeling of obligation, but without any real commitment. When it comes to awakening, which is so radical and different from the "norm", a "Sunday church mentality" won't work. What is required here is a heart-felt commitment.

*As far as not attempting it, there is not much I can do or say about that. However, if you decide to be serious about awakening, I can offer you a very valuable quote by **William Hutchison Murray**, that I had to memorize when I attended business school. It's an exceptional quote to live by on any level and for any undertaking in life. It is especially true and essential to abide by it for awakening, as it requires this kind of commitment. It goes like this:*

"Until one is committed, there is hesitancy, the chance to draw back, always ineffectiveness. CONCERNING ALL ACTS OF INITIATIVE (AND CREATION), THERE IS ONE ELEMENTARY TRUTH, THE IGNORANCE OF WHICH KILLS COUNTLESS IDEAS AND SPLENDID PLANS: THAT THE MOMENT ONE DEFINITELY COMMITS ONESELF, THEN PROVIDENCE MOVES TOO. All sorts of things occur to help one that would never otherwise have occurred. A whole stream of events issues from the decision, raising in one's favour all manner of unforeseen incidents and meetings and material assistance, which no man could have dreamt would have come his way. I have learned a deep respect for one of Goethe's couplets: Whatever you can do, or dream you can, begin it. Boldness has genius, power, and magic in it!"

William Hutchison Murray

Common "Judas Whisper" – "Nothing is Happening"

Question by Martha Rosenthal: *I have been practicing your techniques for a few weeks now, and I must say, they do work... when I actually do them. At times, however, I find myself resisting the practices and don't feel motivated. I don't understand this, since I have always been very disciplined and a highly-motivated person in everything I do. I always see things through and have been very successful in most of my endeavours, whether it be my business or with my music. Please help me understand why this seems so different.*

Gabor: *Yes, Martha. I heard you are a superb violinist. When you are running your business or playing the violin you are motivated to move forward, because these accomplishments fit into your value system and the value system of your peers and surrounding society. Now when it comes to your practice of the techniques that I gave you, the objective of the practice is to take you out of the "time reference reality" and snap you into a "ratio-based reality". However, there is not yet any value established for that. As a matter of fact, your current value system "de-values" this,* *and has no appreciation for it.*

Also, there is no future accomplishment associated with these practices. You are stepping out of an established value system, and yet, you are expecting some kind of evaluation. You are emerging out of the mind-set that would motivate you to practice. Hence, there is no motivation and no future event to move towards.

Martha: *Sometimes I do it, but it feels like nothing is happening.*

Gabor: *First of all, let me remind you that we live in a world where our senses are the ones that pick-up information for us, and the same senses give us feedback as to where we are at, and what is happening. The purpose of the practices I give you is precisely to get you out of the sense world and into the world of non-sense. There is no feedback there. There cannot be any feedback from the world of non-sense to the world of sense.*

> **There is no feedback from the world of non-sense to the world of sense.**

When the organ of unification is activated through the practice of "bypassing" the mind, how could there be feedback from the mind? Here there is no comparing to other experiences or perceptions, but only a sense of unity. From this vantage point, there is no feedback or commentary by the mind. This is no longer the contrast-reality where everything is compared to other things that are different and separate. Here there is only "noticing" and when there is unity, there can't be feedback or comparisons when we are dealing with "oneness".

You might think "I don't get feedback when I do this exercise" or "nothing is happening." It is true that there is no feedback, but it is absolutely NOT true that nothing is happening. Many, many angels and guides are working on your behalf to help you get grounded and anchored into this new reality. Knowing this and being very clear about it, might help you with the thought that says "Nothing is happening." Why would you want to deprive yourself of all these benefits just because your limited senses, which are not capable of picking up signals from "non-sense reality", are telling you that nothing is happening?! Being, or presence, or the higher platform, is running through everything. The senses don't notice it. Only one who is awakened notices this.

Martha: *So what is it that notices it, if it is not the senses?*

Gabor: *Awakening itself is the realization that existence is running through you. Awakening is the moment when Being is recognizing itself. The senses are designed to notice the difference between things. Existence can only be recognized by existence. If the organ that can sense existence is not activated, then how can we sense it?*

Martha: *And which organ is that?*

Gabor: *It is the activated body.*

Martha: *What do you mean by activated body?*

> Many, many angels and guides are working on your behalf to help you get grounded and anchored into this new reality. Why would you want to deprive yourself of all these benefits, just because your limited senses, which are not capable of picking up signals from "non-sense reality" are telling you that nothing is happening?!

Gabor: *When a person exercises his or her "freed will" to turn their attention within, then the body is activated as an existence sensing organ.*

Common "Judas Whisper" – "Help! I Need My Thoughts"

Question by Erik Larsson: *When I practice, sometimes I am full of the fear "How will I survive without thinking?".*

Gabor: *You won't have to survive without thinking! I think as much as is necessary, and I choose what I think. Thinking does not control me. There is a difference between deliberate thinking and what we call "being thought" when thoughts impose themselves on you, grab your attention and compel you to helplessly follow their stream.*

Picking your own thoughts is far superior to having thoughts running through your head and mentally pushing you around. Part of the essence of the teaching is to be able to stop thinking. Once we can do that, we will be able to do deliberate thinking.

> There is a difference between deliberate thinking and what
> we call "being thought", when thoughts impose themselves
> on you, grab your attention, and compel you to helplessly
> follow their stream.

Erik: *But I heard in some of your lectures, that you cannot actually stop the thoughts. So how do I reconcile that with stopping the thoughts so that I will think deliberately?*

Gabor: *Here is where we can start getting used to paradoxes – we have to stop the thought stream, but we cannot stop it. When we successfully apply the technique of "bypassing", the thought will slow down or even stop. The "smart wheel" thinking cannot be shut down or turned off in the same way that we shut our eyes, or cover our ears. We cannot control thinking in the same way that we do with the senses. The only way we can stop the thinking is by "bypassing" the thinking mechanism entirely, which is what we do when we activate the body as a transformational organ, through awakening.*

Once we can do this with ease, and we can default to the space of "no thought", we are able to choose the thoughts that are useful to us, and eventually, the contrast-reality mind becomes comfortable in the role of a servant. At this point it will no longer want to take control. It will be happy serving you in a way that is much more efficient than it ever could before - when it was motivated by fear and greed.

Common "Judas Whisper" – "Stop Taking Away my Fun"

Question by Michael Grange: *I feel like you are raining on my spiritual parade. You have taken away all my spiritual fun of visions, astral traveling and other exciting spiritual experiences.*

Gabor: *Yes, it seems that way to the limited mind. Remember, we were created with many God-like abilities that are factory-built in, and the two most significant ones are:*

a. The "contrast-reality" interface, which is our ability to interact with our world by making distinctions, comparing, analysing, drawing conclusions, creating mental templates etc. in this world of contrasts.

b. The "ratio-reality" interface, which is our ability to interact with the world, by seeing it as it **IS** and uniting with it.

As we know, the currently limited mind is very much interconnected with the senses. Everything that the senses perceive is interpreted, compared, analysed, stored away or acted on by the mind. Today's meditation experience is compared immediately to the one we had yesterday, and a conclusion is drawn that it is better, or not as good as... and therefore me must....

Even so-called spiritual experiences, such as visions, are all triggered by one's existing spiritual and cultural templates. If you have a catholic background you might be stimulated to see Jesus or Mother Mary; with a Hindu upbringing, you may have visions of Krishna or Lord Maitreya etc. All these experiences are passed through the mind for inspection and comparisons, and are considered to be great milestones towards enlightenment, which are stored away as profound advancements on the path. Then of course, they are piled onto one's spiritual egoic identity, as being "more spiritual than others and therefore, one is more suitable for becoming a powerful spiritual teacher."

These experiences contribute greatly to the delusion called mysticism, that forever keeps the future event we so strive for, at arm's length. For all we know, those visions could be none other than an encounter of pareidolia. (Pareidolia is a psychological phenomenon involving a stimulus - an image or a sound - wherein the mind perceives a familiar pattern of something, where none exist). But remember, for the purpose of awakening, we must tear down the pedestal of mystery and allow the elevated platform of living to be present and interwoven in every part of our day-to-day living, no matter how mundane we imagine it to be.

As I said before, currently, in this contrast-reality, we are aware of and interpret only 0.1% of reality. Even when we have visions with closed eyes which we consider to be "inner", in some cases this might be "inner pareidolia". In the dream state and in the linear type of meditation,

> For awakening to occur we must tear down the pedestal of mystery, and allow the elevated platform of living to be present and interwoven in every part of our day-to-day living, no matter how mundane we imagine it to be.

all our experiences are still in the mind. Whether good, bad, relaxed or spiritual – they are all states of mind and therefore, they are interpreted by the contrast-reality limitations. So visions are mostly advanced delusions and generally, they are NOT an indication of being close to awakening.

So it may feel like I am taking away your spiritual fun, but this must be done, since we can only get through the "eye of the needle" when we are totally naked... when all our spiritual/mental cloaks are removed. The **GOOD NEWS** *is that immeasurable fun, magic, miracles, colorful experiences, "super- powers" and more are waiting for you right around the corner. Once you have entered the new platform and are anchored in it, in that context you may enjoy any number of experiences without being dragged back to mind-based spirituality.*

> We can only get through the "eye of the needle", when we are totally naked... when all our spiritual/mental cloaks are removed.

Why get stuck in a limited playground... ?

When you can have unlimited fun in the universal playground!

"I Wish It Wasn't So!" – The Judas Stockholm Syndrome

Many seekers unknowingly fall victim to search addiction. They have been hijacked by the contrast-based mind that has sent them on a life-long wild-goose chase after an elusive and unachievable goal: to find the "Self" that has never been lost in the first place. This obsession eventually becomes enjoyable since it allows one to develop a new self-image and a sense of importance that feels much more secure than any "unknown".

Now the seeker who has been kidnapped by his/her own mind, becomes trapped in the "Judas Stockholm Syndrome". (Stockholm Syndrome is a condition that causes hostages to develop a psychological alliance with their captors as a survival strategy during captivity.) In spite of the desire to be free which has lead him/her to an awakening path, there is a deep-seated reluctance to move out of the comfort zone of the new self-image and to relinquish the familiar "captor/mind".

By some grace this victim has stumbled upon the path of true awakening and suddenly he/she "gets" the feeling that turning within and activating the transformational body is **"THE END OF THE LINE!"**. This "end" is what is feared the most by "seeking addicts". They reluctantly intuit that beyond this point, there is no more searching, analysing, comparing or "efforting". In spite of the inner evidence that this "is it", the addiction to the restlessness, the anticipation and the expected rewards of the "search" are still lingering and trying to survive. There is an inner sensation that this compulsion is about to die and there is nothing one can do about it.

This is very much like a healing crisis or the feeling of "die off" that one experiences during the process of detoxification. Thus, the subconscious whisper "I wish it wasn't so" begins to take over and it is usually accompanied by frantically researching other gurus who teach "pseudo awakening". The subconscious feeling goes something like this: "I want to do this awakening thing, but I want to find a path that will allow me to keep having ongoing exciting experiences and sign posts that show me how much I am advancing."

The real motivation behind this thought, that is totally concealed and unrecognized, is the mind's desperate attempt to become re-empowered by being allowed to participle in the process, so that it can remain on the throne and perhaps even take the credit for a so-called spiritual attainment. This is rarely noticed by the student at first. It is only when an awakening guide points this out, that one may recognize this tendency.

> **The last thing that the mind wants one to realize is that "searching" is ALWAYS done by the contrast-mind and therefore, is the biggest obstacle to awakening.**

Question by Linda Jones: I've heard you say that at some point after awakening, the mind starts to rebel and tries to get one out of this unfamiliar territory and back into past memories and future fears and desires, in order to regain its control. Did you experience that as well?

Gabor: It was a bit different for me. Having gone through so many years of suicidal depression, my mind was already extremely beaten up. Therefore, the new platform that I discovered was a great break. Finding it felt like an enormous victory and my mind was more willing to settle into it, rather than continue with its previous madness.

From my experience of working with many people, I now realize that this is not always the case. When there is not much suffering prior to one's awakening, often times, the mind will not give in so easily. This is where the teachings come in, so that hopefully, students won't have to suffer by going through shocking events, and so that their minds can accept simplicity without tremendous pain. Please excuse the generalization in my attempts to explain the unexplainable.

The Healing Crisis

For most people life is not a walk in the park. I don't know anyone who has not suffered one disappointment or another: the loss of a loved one, poverty, heart-break, humiliation, failure etc. This is all part of the contrast-based reality that we live in. There are few who know how to use these situations to leap out of this dimension. Not too many are able to resolve the countless hits and struggles for survival without developing the "protective mechanism" that works hard on our behalf. It relentlessly suppresses our emotions and guards us against future hurts by instilling in us fear, worry and restraint, resulting in stifled behaviour. This is all natural and in many cases, it helps us get through life - not alive, of course - but semi-unscathed.

During our integration process many bottled-up emotions, unpleasant feelings and stored injuries begin to surface in order to be released. They may manifest in various ways such as extreme distress, intense fear, depression, stirred up painful emotions and memories, and even physical illness. Nonetheless, they are not here to hurt us. They are not our enemies that we must fight against and get rid of. We must recognize their significance as co-catalysts. We have the chance to use these emerging emotions as catalysts that help us go deeper into "Beingness" and we become a catalyst for them so that they can be freed. The techniques of "bypassing" and using our "freed will" that are discussed in previous chapters work very well with this kind of healing crisis.

Don't try to "fix" the catalyst! It is your best friend!

HOME SWEET HOME

The "Freedom Point" - The Point of No Return

The "Freedom Point" on the "Integration Curve" is where the "Judas Curve" ends. If the "Judas Curve" with all its whispers did not kick us off the path of awakening, we have completed our "rite of passage" and we are well on our way to complete integration.

It doesn't mean the integration is now 100% complete, but enough of our life has been integrated that the magnetic field of the "smart wheels" and the "Judas Curve" will no longer affect us. We are now like the rocket that has left the magnetic field of the earth and goes into orbit. There is no more pull in the direction of the contrast-reality. There is no resistance, and it is easy to go inside. Being inside, or what I call "In-bodiment", is now our default place. We are HOME and are equally comfortable in the contrast-reality as well as in the ratio-based reality.

There is now a perfect interface between the two realities. We can regulate which reality we wish to be in and work with. We are God-Man realized. This is the point of life after activation. I like the word activation, since it is not mysterious or mystical. We could use all kinds of words from Sanskrit, like Moksha, but that would make this experience appear mystical and unusual, which it is not.

The avalanche of events that lead to self-realization has been triggered by the use of your "freed will" and you recognize that the mind never really was the culprit. It always had the so-called "missing abilities", but it required the spark of activation for those abilities to be realized. The mind is a self-evolving, self-limiting, self-regulating, self-dividing, self-proportioning and self-angling multi-dimensional interface. When it is inter-woven with the body's intelligence, it contains within itself the possibility of self-awareness. Knowing this is true **FREEDOM!**

And so, we now see clearly the difference between "noticing" and comparing. Our mind's abilities have been activated, and this allows us to notice what is needed to be noticed, without having it run its usual habit of comparing, labeling, compartmentalizing etc.

The *MIND* is a self-evolving, self-limiting, self-regulating, self-dividing, self-proportioning and self-angling multi-dimensional interface.

Once the self-angling ability has been activated, and the mind is inter-woven with the body's intelligence, it will have the possibility of self-awareness.

"Integration" – Amalgamating Realities

As is shown in diagram 14, the "Integration Curve" begins at the "portal" and continues on for as long as is necessary. It includes the "Honeymoon Curve" and the "Judas Curve" and passes the "Freedom Point", until one has fully integrated the ratio-based reality with every aspect of life. There really is no end to it, as there is no end to life... as long as we are in form. Basically, once we enter the portal, we are always integrating, as long as our attention is pulled in, as in "IN-bodiment". It just gets a lot easier, once we reach the "Freedom Point", since there is no more pull from the magnetic field of the "smart wheels".

In reality, there is no such point as the "Freedom Point" or time allocated for completing integration. At this point, none of the above are in time. We are just explaining it this way so that the mind can comprehend the best it can. In the "Integration Curve", we learn to live in the world, yet not be of the world. The linear reality of time is going on and all the timed events in the contrast-reality are happening, while we keep bringing our attention to the ratio-based reality.

This is where the practice of re-proportioning our attention must be engaged. We use our greatest asset, namely our attention, and with our "freed will" we look and feel within the body while retaining some of our attention outside, in order to deal with the world around us and function properly.

Integration is the reconciling of the contrast-reality information and events with - or rather **INTO** – the ratio-based reality. Remember, integration only occurs as we are in the IN-bodiment mode. So for example, we may have a problem or some negative information, or even exciting information, in the contrast-reality. When we are Being Present, we are able to embrace, engulf and simply BE with whatever information comes to us from the contrast-reality. In doing so, we integrate it into the ratio-based reality, in which we reside as we are present.

My New Unconditionally Nurturing Base

Question by Linda Jones: So, once you were awake, what was your integration like? How did you go about living in both realities?

Gabor: When you are walking in a forest and there is no need to pay attention to people or to think, then you can allow yourself to sink into this nurturing place by doing nothing. It takes no extra effort to go deeper and deeper into presence. It just requires a minor intention. When there is no demand on you to function in life, you can quite easily go into what people imagine Nirvana to be.

In my case, I had a construction project in Mexico to complete and so the integration of what I had found into my everyday life had to be accelerated. I couldn't afford to sit on a mountain top and meditate, or see the world with rose colored glasses and bliss out. I was quickly forced to face the harsh realities of the world from my new platform and learn to function from there.

This was a welcomed challenge. There was no longer a need to escape. I now had the ability to live out from a consistent, unconditional and nurturing base. I was like a kid with a new toy. "Ok, what do I do with this toy?" was my new consideration. It was an experimental phase. I knew it worked, but now I was learning how to make it work while functioning in what I used to consider a dysfunctional world.

So I tried it while speaking with strangers on the street, in busy market places and in dealing with bureaucrats, whom I loathed throughout my earlier life. It was amazing to be able to shift the depth of my presence on demand. How wonderful to find that, although the stressful thoughts of speaking with some of these officials and administrators were still there on the surface, speaking with them from my new nurturing space, was like pushing the clutch in a standard car and disengaging the thoughts and narratives that have plagued me in the past. Now, this is freedom!

I also began using this while working out. I found that when I did my curls or bench presses to the point where I felt the "burn" in the muscles, as long as I was in my body and staying in my new space of stillness, the sensation in the muscles was still there, but there was no suffering. The mind was pleased to be in its peaceful and secure home and had no need to bring up its usual negative chronicle that habitually accompanied pain.

Integrating the Freedom of Functional Silence

Linda: And what was freedom like for you at this point?

Gabor: Nothing at all like I previously expected it to be. Now there was a vague memory that I'd been here before during times of crisis or shock, but there was also the feeling that BEING HERE is my default mode. I realized that there was no other practice needed. Any other practice, including and especially the cultivation of spiritual attributes and behaviours, felt inferior when compared to the simple delving into this nurturing well.

I now began to see things as they are. I started to view the world AS

> I started to view the world AS IT IS, as opposed to the way my mind described it through the filters of its former good or bad memories and inflicted fears and needs.

IT IS, as opposed to the way my mind described it through the filters of its former good or bad memories and inflicted fears and needs. For example, when I meet someone from my past, I still have the full recollection of them, but this memory is fully integrated into the stillness and the presence of my new platform.

Therefore, every moment I am able to look at them with fresh eyes. The memories are no longer assumptive, nor do they colour what I feel and say, or how I deal with a particular person at the moment I am with him/her.

The question of judgment or forgiveness does not even arise. I can listen to people without bias and without having my mind run its own interfering story. I don't wait for people to shut up so that I can say what I want. I am never in a "desperately waiting" mode. I am just BEING with them, while remaining in the nurturing place of inner silence, which is the only way to truly hear and bless anyone. This is why, prior to awakening, cultivating spiritual attributes such as forgiveness, compassion, non-judgement etc. are futile, and they only contribute to the enhancement of one's spiritual ego.

If and when I do need an informational thought form from the past in order to handle a life situation, I can simply pull it off the shelf and use it on demand. Now I am in control of the mind and I am no longer pushed around by it. The mind has a new home in which it can relax, and it doesn't have to put so much effort into protecting me from attacks, or fulfilling my survival needs. It no longer has the necessity to steal energy from others or to fear the unknown. The thought forms and skills acquired in the past are now integrated into a nurturing context.

In my earlier life, my mind didn't have this secure and supportive base, which is why it acted so crazy and kept searching for escapes to better places and improved situations. Now freedom is established by inner nurturing, not outer. It is constant, loving and not at all mysterious. For this reason, I also feel exceptionally good with "not knowing". My mind has lost its constant craving to know, to be in control and to figure everything out. When I have a question, I sit with it and "BE" with it. Sooner or later answers start flooding in from the center of my being, untainted by thoughts that are derivative, analytical and inferior mental concepts.

Freedom has been established by inner nurturing, not outer!

My mind has lost its constant craving to know, to be in control and to figure everything out.

How to Make Future Plans While Being in the "Now"?

Linda: *So, when you live in the "now", how do you go about making plans for the Future?*

Gabor: *It is very correct to ask this question, since there is a built-in conflict with it – two "time" references – the "now" and the "future". First of all, we have to examine what we mean by the "now". The only reason the "now" exists, is because the past and the future exist. In actuality, "now" does not have its own existence. It only exists in relation to the past and the future.*

The "now" is a time-based expression. When we are addressing a piece of information, we are using our freshly activated ability to shift into a ratio-based reference. So, the expression "We have to be in the 'now'" is really inaccurate. We are not going into the "now". We only used that expression temporarily. The "now" is a perspective of a time-based observer.

We need to address the future plans from a ratio-based reality perspective, and not from a time-based perspective. In other words, I am here in the ratio-reality. I am not in the "now". From this ratio-based reality perspective, I take the template called "future planning" off the shelf. I work with this template to create a future plan. When I finish, I put it back on the shelf. By the way, you have no idea how well your future plans will work out, when making them from the ratio-reality perspective.

> If I am not <u>in</u> the "time-based" reality, but only working with it, while I am <u>in</u> the "no-time" ratio-based reality, there is no conflict in making future plans.

We allow the expression "being in the 'now'" for the sake of bringing the people who are new to awakening to get to a certain level of understanding, and to release the practice that is attached to a future event. As part of the integration, we have to bring people to a different level of understanding in which the "now", as a time-based reality expression, can be transcended into the ratio-based reality, where it is given a new expression.

As I said before, in each new "level", the words and the steps that preceded are discarded, as they are no longer relevant in the new phase. As we move on, we must transcend our own expressions.

Linda: *Wow... not sure if I get this. For the past 20 years, I was under the impression that the past and the future are illusions and that only the "now" is real.*

Gabor: *We are dealing here with an evolution of terms. It is a matter of semantics. More importantly, it is a matter of who is looking. Are we looking at this from the contrast-based reality viewpoint or are we attempting to talk about it from the golden ratio reality perspective?*

You've heard me speak of the "The Mirage on the Other Side of the Fence". On the other side of the fence, which is the golden ratio reality, there is only Being. Looking at it from the contrast-reality perspective, an awakened person looks like the opposite of any personal trait that we want to modify. If we are addressing any kind of negative behavior like judgment, impatience etc., an enlightened being appears to be the opposite of that – accepting, patient etc. However, this is an error. This assumption only exists in the contrast-reality mind. Hence, I call this supposition "The Mirage on the Other Side of the Fence".

The same is true when it comes to time-based terminology. In the contrast-based reality that we live in we speak in terms of time and have suitable words for this time-based reality. When we look at awakened people on the other side of the fence, it seems as though they are in the "now". Since their minds are not running with past and future thoughts, memories and anticipations, we assume they must be in the "now". We conclude that on the other side of the fence the past and the future are nothing but illusions and that only the "now" is real. This conclusion is also an error.

On the other side of the fence, in the golden ratio reality, there is no contrast-based or time-based reality. And therefore, there is no time-based expression. There is just Being. From this perspective, none of the time-based terms are accurate, including the "now". That is why I say that the "now" is a timed-based expression and it only exists as long as the past and future exist.

Orbiting - the "Freedom Point"

Leaving earth's magnetic field through IN-bodiment.

The "lift-off" ignited by free will.

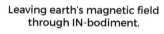

BENEDICTION

Whether you are spiritually exhausted or a novice, it is my sincere hope and prayer that reading this book has done for you what it was intended to do:

-tear down the veils of spiritual delusion

-take the mystery of lineage off its pedestal

-remove the beliefs that awakening is only for a select few

-expose the cunning nature of the personal and collective minds

-de-mystify awakening

-create a clear distinction between true awakening and spirituality

-give you the courage to claim your birthright - awakening!

-immunize you against the opinions of the masses and unawakened teachers

-convince you that awakening cannot happen through a mind-path

-help you recognize the value of simplicity

-activate a desire within in you to go HOME

If the universe has been pushing you in the direction of awakening by throwing difficulties along your path, you may have been feeling as though the "cards of life" have been stacked **against** you. My benediction/wish for you is that by opening up to true awakening and embracing the abundant gifts it holds, you will now realize that the "cards of life" are, always have been and always will be "stacked **FOR** you".

> It is my firm conviction, that even a miniscule amount of effort of going within can and does yield great results. May you share this conviction with me through your own experience.

IMPRESSIONS AND IMPACTS

By Iain McNay

I enjoyed very much meeting and interviewing Gabor. It is always really inspiring to meet someone who has had such a challenging path and in spite of so many obstacles, is able to find peace and wisdom and finally start to rest in the ground of being. I felt that with Gabor.

Iain McNay, founder of Conscious.TV (London, UK)

By Stefan Hiene

When I had the privilege of looking into Gabor's eyes, I looked into the eyes of an ageless child, the eyes of innocence. The child within me felt totally seen with unconditional love. No story, no judgment, just this very pure moment. I feel blessed to know Gabor and Nurit. They are treasures of pureness.

Stefan Hiene, author, spiritual mentor and coach (Stuttgart, Germany)

By Boudewijn Zweerts

Along the complex and difficult paths of truth-finding, the yet unexperienced, non-dual perception of reality and the slow realisation that my mind is not going to make it... I found Gabor pointing to and talking with our famous interviewer Ian McNay of Conscious TV. The good fortune I had to meet him in person has been a gift and confirmation that indeed, everything is energy.

Before the moment we actually met, I already sensed his presence on the street, though I couldn't find him immediately. The calmness that comes from his being or energy field is already a blessing to receive. We then talked, where he shared the insights gained in his life. This, my mind needed, and my heart said "YES" in a sigh of relief. "Just BE... pay attention with awareness to what's going on inside the corpus, around the heart, underneath the mind. Not once, but as much as possible... and that's it!"

Thank you, Gabor, for giving me the tools and context to know why. All the best to you, readers! After having read Gabor's work, you will know what you need to know.

Boudewijn Zweerts, BSc, founder of Sounds of Silence (The Netherlands)

By Jann Gougeon

My spiritual search started as a result of an amazing experience of oneness, peace and the absence of fear, that happened thirty years ago and was the catalyst that sparked my long and determined search through many, many avenues of spirituality (transcendental and other forms of meditation; CIM; 8 years of the International Pathwork Foundation; Anthroposophy; Theosophy; dozens of metaphysical and spiritual books).

After many years of being the proverbial spiritual seeker, I finally dropped the books and the internet became my tool, which is where I first saw Gabor Harsanyi's interview on Conscious TV. I was never one to give my "power" up to a guru or sit transfixed at anyone's feet. My intention in listening to the many guests on Conscious TV was to discover if a "regular person" like me could wake up.

Gabor's message resonated, as it was simple and it made sense to me. There was no nonduality terminology or philosophical, intellectual, psychological discourse... no guru lineages. I was done with that. I wanted simple, practical direction. I sensed he was the "real deal".

Gabor is present. His direction cuts through all the spiritual "lingo" I had developed in my search. I was amazed to find that all the "knowledge" I had accumulated was the very thing that prevented me from realizing my inner longing.

In the many sessions I have had with Gabor, Presence has always come through in all his guidance. From the beginning, I experienced his genuineness, integrity, honesty, generosity and delightful humor, as well as the energetic resonance of an awakened being. I feel so blessed for having sent him that first email, as I have found the inner peace I was seeking, and it continues to deepen by using his simple tools. Thank you, Gabor!

Jann Gougeon, artist, B.S. psychology, Energy Healer (Michigan, USA)

By Attila Hack

Gabor's guidance did not feed my spiritual intellect... it rather deepened my connection with my own universal essence (God).

Attila Hack, Hotel Manager (Northern England)

By Pierre Richard

I've known Gabor Harsanyi for over a year and I come away from each of his sessions feeling elated and expanded. It's such a pleasure, and he brings the best out of me... I experience my deepest nature in his presence. Gabor is a rare teacher, who transmits wisdom through laughter. He's totally down to earth and much like your next-door neighbor, except that he can cut through old conditioning and beliefs with radical precision.

His practices are clear and simple. For myself, spiritual talk that doesn't include tangible insights that can be applied to my own life, is not inspiring. Gabor goes beyond concepts and philosophy! This is his force and he cuts through to the heart.

Pierre Richard, Musician (Montréal, Canada)

By György Liptovszky

For so long I have been searching for a path to enlightenment, that is feasible in our fast-paced lives in this 21st Century. The days of contemplating in the silence of a cave are obviously over. Where are those silent caves today? Even if we were to find one, there would most likely be at least three people in them, already sitting there, meditating on their sleeping bags ...

For quite some time, I felt that the only suitable path would be one that requires constant inner attention, and to live our everyday life with that attention. Therefore, I tried to be on the path of the Jesus Prayer, and later lived with the inner sound (Nada) for many years. I prayed to the Universe to send me a helper, a master who can guide me ...... as no one had real experiences with these methods. Some have read about them and tried to share their experiences with me. However, I constantly longed for a master who could teach this, from the light of enlightenment.

After 15 years, my unspoken prayers were answered, when I met Gabor. At the first moment, I knew that he taught exactly what I had been waiting for: the continuity of presence, in a simple, practical, playful and surprising way.

Having read all spiritual literature from A to Z, I arrogantly thought that no one could teach me anything new. However, now I spend many hours with Gabor, and I am constantly filled with new and significant realizations, surprises and joy. What he says is new, different, fresh and exhilarating! When we finish a session, I can hardly wait for the next opportunity to meet him. Every sentence is so important, that I never have time to ask about his personal life. I just drink the timeless knowledge that emanates from him.

Gabor can perfectly guide anyone on this pathless-path, until the recognition dawns that all the necessary paths have already been roamed, and there is only one more step to take!

György Liptovszky, Strategic Director (Geneva, Switzerland)

By Andras Petz

Simplicity! That was the word that gripped my heart and interrupted my mind, when I heard Gabor's speech in a public session. Even in my work as a computer programmer, I realized that the most sophisticated programs that actually work well, are simple. In private sessions with Gabor, I truly experienced that his "teachings" and "exercises" are really simple and easy, IF one is humble and "flexible" enough to follow.

I have stopped all my readings about esoteric and religious topics long ago. I have yearned to experience the truth that all those books talk about. Interestingly, in the past, I had always degraded my body and considered it to be insignificant. However, with Gabor's help, I now know that the body is not my enemy; it is the "gate". My search is finally over! I realize that Gabor's teachings are what I had been looking for. After my first private session with Gabor I experienced the "aliveness" and the depth of his teachings. We were sitting in a coffee shop, and suddenly, the sounds around me changed and I felt an indescribable calm without any thoughts.

There are no words to express this state, but I recognized immediately that this is the root of existence. It was not a trans state. I was totally aware of my surroundings and I was able to act much more efficiently when it was needed. My speech became slower, deeper and fuller, as well as more precise and filled with the "force" (a la Star Wars!).

After my initial realization, I became aware of the importance of integration, which is an essential part of Gabor's teachings. Gabor is not an advocate of becoming a hermit, who lives in a monastery. On the contrary! He urges one to continue living one's life with family and job. I learned too, that in the integration phase, it is up to me to apply my free will, my birthright. The keys that I now know and have adopted are: applying the free will, listening to my inner self through my body that is deeply connected with the root of existence, and caressing the moment.

Andras Petz, computer programmer (Budapest, Hungary)

By Birgitta Süss

For me Gabor is a guide, who leads me through the jungle of my inner world and shows me the path that brings me home again. In my days of suffering and emotional upheaval, where I seemed to have been locked in for so long, he has given me very effective tools and has helped me shift my awareness in the direction of freedom, peace, love, joy and stillness. These are but a few of the new feelings that I have now experienced in the new life, that Gabor has opened for me.

He always works with me like a dear friend, who never judges and always listens with patience and care. He has been like a father and a mother, who are right beside me, feeling what I am feeling, holding my hand and BEING with me every step of the way.

Birgitta Süss (Ottensheim, Austria)

By Dorina Dumitrescu

I was not at the beginning of my "spiritual" journey, when Grace brought me to the Hungarian Master of Silence - Gabor Harsanyi. On the contrary. I had encountered two masters before – a transcendental meditation (TM) teacher and a shaman. During this time, I had various experiences and I also began dealing with illness, pain and weakness in the body, which has been going on for about 30 years, even though all my medical check-ups showed that everything was fine.

I was fed up with life and was having negative and depressing thoughts of illness, while a part of me was still able to bear this with acceptance. I call this the "deadlock phase" of my journey, before meeting Gabor.

My former master has endowed me with a warrior spirit and an enduring spirit. He instilled in me the understanding that, "All that happens is your doing... your programming. There is no one to help you but yourself, and you do this through acceptance and forgiveness." Thus, in this "deadlock phase", I did not go seeking for help, but rather prayed for months to my soul, to either activate my inner Master to take me out of this unbearable phase - or to bring me a new master who would continue to guide me from this point.

Well, my prayer was answered! One day, among the many spiritual teachers I was listening to on a daily basis, I was instantly drawn to Gabor, after hearing Nurit's (Gabor's wife) story about him. I watched several of Gabor's videos. I immediately decided to write to him and start one-on-one sessions. As I write this testimonial, I see that I have gotten out of the 'deadlock phase,' and I owe this to Gabor's guidance. What was the magic of Gabor?

For the 1st time in my spiritual journey, I've received some clear "tools"! These were not meditation or mantra repetition, which I have grown tired of, and which did not help me during my problem phase. These new "tools" enabled me to cope with the pain and pressure and, oddly enough, be happy when those occurred.

Gabor has passed this information to me in a very precise, clear and gentle manner. He should be called not only the Master of Silence, but also the Master of Precision. Listening to him and following his guidance, pain was no longer an "enemy", or something you have to endure as a sacrifice, but rather as "your baby"- as Gabor says – "that should be welcomed, embraced, listened to, rocked and loved."

This tool was instantly embraced and recognized as true by my whole being. I feel it was a sort of "transmission" - beyond the mere words - that comes from a true master. I must say, that with this master, my picky and very critical mind was left with nothing to comment on in the face of these obvious results. It was reduced to silence.

The 2nd tool was the focusing of attention in the body. Again, this came with instant results of calmness, silence of the body and mind and "moment to moment-ness".

Gabor listens with immense patience, respect and non-judgment to any nonsense one may utter to him. He clearly has the gift/power to identify any problem underneath or behind the words, and come up with the exact guidance that is needed at the moment for that person. He knows what one's biggest weakness/shadow/challenge is that must be faced, and when it comes to guidance, he never imposes or forces anything. He really does not have to, since you end up doing it anyway, by recognizing the truth behind his teachings.

Only a true master, a person who has crossed the path and has realized the truth, can impact others – without boasting, without forcing, with simple and precise words and with mere silence. This describes Gabor, even though the words are mere pointers and not the reality itself.

Another possible "name" for Gabor is the "Fine-tuning Master". As one's experience unfolds by integrating Gabor's teachings, one gets from him exactly the very thing/explanation/words that one needs to 'perfect' one's experience. This is the very polishing you need to make sure, once more, that you got it right.

To sum up: Among the masters on my path, Gabor came along to do the refined work. His teachings are invaluable to me! He has pulled me from a hollow place, where I was sitting as a victim of bodily pain and depression, and showed me the power inside. He led me to unleash it and feel complete. He enabled me to live what before was a mere statement - that all we need is inside us. The world is the same, but I look at it differently. Nature, and especially the trees, are my friends and gentle presences, that are perceived without the filter of the mind.

Hafiz's poem below resembles Gabor's way of dealing with students and, consequently, his impact upon them:

'Even

After

All this time

The Sun never says to the Earth,

"You owe me."

Look

What happens

With a love like that,

It lights the whole sky.' — **Hafiz**

Dorina Dumitrescu, author, lawyer (Bucharest, Romania)

"FORGET-ME-NOT" DEFINITIONS

4th Progression

The area of "entry" through the "Golden Ratio Gate" where the golden ratio begins. At this place, that we are calling the 4th progression, there is no longer a linear progression. Here there is no progression, but a "leap". Although from the 4th progression on, we can enter the "Golden Ratio Gate", or the golden ratio reality, we cannot "continue" into it. We must "leap" into it! We must "leap" out of the contrast-reality into the 4th progression at an angle. This is a point of leaping, angling, surrendering. This is where the mind begins to acquire its angling abilities.

Aha Gates

The "Aha Gates" are a metaphor for the gates of understanding and functionality on a mental or intellectual level, that we enter on the third dimensional living. Whenever a certain attainment has been achieved or an important realization has been reached, we have our "Aha" moments, in which we feel and think, "Aha! Aha! Now I know!" We then move "up" to the next step/level, as we enter the next gate of accumulated knowledge.

Angular Leap

An angular leap is what is necessary for leaping out of the contrast-reality and entering the "Golden Ratio Gate" at the 4th progression, where there is no longer a linear progression. At the 4th progression we can enter the "Golden Ratio Gate", or the golden ratio reality, not through a "continuity" into it, but rather, via a leap that is at an angle to life's linearity. An angular leap is akin to an act of humbly surrendering and leaping to the dimensionless dimension beyond the 3rd dimension of duality existence. This is where the mind begins to acquire its angling abilities, and this is what all our practices are based on.

Arany Kapu

In Magyar Arany Kapu (pronounced 'aran-kapoo') means the Golden Gate. By adding an apostrophe-like sign on top of the second "a", we get "Arány Kapu", which means "Golden Ratio Gate". It is the Golden Gate, which also means that it is the "Golden Ratio Gate" and the ratio itself contains the key to the "how to" in order to open the gate and access HOME.

Awakening

Awakening is the ability to "bypass" the mind's participation when necessary. It is the moment when Being is recognizing itself.

Bypassing

"Bypassing" refers to side-stepping the mind instead of wrestling with it, in order to make it stop controlling us. By "bypassing" I don't mean ignoring the mind/problem or shoving it under the carpet. It is rather a turning within and dealing with things from an inner-bodily elevated platform, with no mind interference, adjudication or evaluation. We practice "bypassing" systems, and NOT "lighten-the-load" systems. This is done by pulling in our attention and placing it in the body, thus initiating the re-activation of the body as a transformational organ.

Once we are aligned with the intelligence of the body, which is equivalent to the entire ratio-based universe, we are on a whole different platform and we become aware of the interwoven-ness of the universe. The moment we are aware of this interwoven-ness, the mind is automatically "bypassed" as it loses its hold on us in this realm.

The key in the practice of "bypassing" is to enter the activated body (which is the no-thought realm) immediately... as soon the need to "bypass" an unwanted thought is noticed. If not, the mind will always jump in right away with its "smart" attempts to "fix" the problem through thinking.

Chewed Up Bones

Chewed up bones are repetitive words that have been so over-used that they have lost their meaning and lustre.

Contrast-reality

Contrast-reality is our world of duality. Its objects and concepts are recognized and referenced through their opposites - hate is hate, since it is not love; dark is dark since it is not light etc.

Egy

In the ancient language of Magyar, Egy (pronounced 'edge') means one or ONENESS.

Elevated Platform

The elevated platform is the dimensionless dimension, beyond the duality of the contrast-reality we live in. It is where the concepts of "good or bad", "happy or sad", "functional or dysfunctional" etc. become irrelevant, and no longer have a hold on us. This is true FREEDOM!

Fibonacci Numbers

Nature's numbering system is called the Fibonacci numbers. This is how nature builds, as was discovered by Italian mathematician, Fibonacci. These numbers are: 1, 2, 3, 5, 8, 13, 21, 34, 55, 89, 144... etc. Starting from number "5" there is a ratio of 1.61 between all these numbers.

Freed Will

This is the evolved free will, when the will has become free of thoughts, expectations and the influence of the sense/fear-based templates. Freed will is the human ability to focus the attention within the body, even though there is absolutely no motivation to do so from the mind and from society as a whole. (I mean "actually" feeling inside and not just talking about it!)

Freedom Point

The "Freedom Point" on the "Integration Curve" is where the "Judas Curve" ends. If the "Judas Curve" with all its whispers did not kick us off the path of awakening, we have completed our "rite of passage", and we are well on our way to complete integration. Here the magnetic field of the "smart wheels" and the "Judas Curve" will no longer affect us. There is no more pull in the direction of the contrast-reality. There is no resistance, and it is easy to go inside. Being inside, or what I call "In-bodiment", is now our default place. We are HOME and are equally comfortable in the contrast-reality as well as in the ratio-based reality.

Functional Silence

The ability to live and function from the elevated platform of Being. When inner silence is the base of our being and we are able to function in contrast-reality from that space, we are the living evidence of "Functional Silence".

Golden Ratio Gate

The "Golden Ratio Gate" is a metaphor for the entry into the realm of Silence, or what we call the "Elevated Platform of Living". It is what Jesus referred to as the entry through the eye of the needle. This is where the domain of the golden ratio begins and the contrast-based reality ends.

Golden Ratio

The golden ratio is the ratio of 1 to 1.61 that the human body, as well as every measurement, expansion and growth in nature, is based on. The Universe was not created in a linear manner, but rather in a logarithmic spiral fashion and with this ratio.

Honeymoon Curve

The "Honeymoon Curve" is a short segment that begins at the "portal". In this phase one is amazed and often excited about the new-found peace and silence. There is a quality/non-quality to this silence that is unlike anything that belongs to the spiritual world that springs from the "Aha Gates". It is a wonderful segment of discovery and the practices are engaged with full fervour and curiosity.

Igen

The Magyar word "Igen" (pronounced 'eeg-en') in day-to-day life means "yes". It also exists in the word "intell-igen-ce". Igen is a coded word that is carried forth in the Magyar language. In its coded format, it is a seed word or a central word, very much like the cog of a wheel, from which all kinds of essential truths are derived. It offers the beginning of a new world in which, once entered, there is the possibility of true intelligence.

IN-Bodiment

IN-bodiment means to actually sense the inner vitality of the body and live from that platform of existence.

Inner Silence

Inner silence is the cessation of all mental traffic, where one is no longer being "thought" by the mind but, rather in full control of his/her thought stream. Inner silence is not the opposite of noise. It has as much in common with outer silence as a butterfly has in common with the butterfly strokes of a swimmer.

Integration Curve

The "Integration Curve" begins at the "portal" and continues on for as long as is necessary. It includes the "Honeymoon Curve" and the "Judas Curve" and passes the "Freedom Point", until one has fully integrated the ratio-based reality with every aspect of life. There really is no end to it, as there is no end to life... as long as we are in form. Basically, once we awaken we are always integrating, as long as our attention is pulled in as in "IN-bodiment". It does get a lot easier once we reach the "Freedom Point", since there is no more pull from the magnetic field of the "smart wheels".

Judas Curve

The "Judas Curve" is a phase that starts at the "portal" and ends at the "Freedom Point". This is the segment where one is still pulled by the magnetic field of one's templates and the "smart wheel" propensities of the "Aha Gates" which can cause one to fall prey to any of the contrast-reality's tempting distractions. This is where one might betray one's self and give up on awakening, justifying this with all kinds of brilliant and "sensible" excuses and pretexts.

Magyar

Magyar (pronounced 'madge-yar') is an ancient language that contains the main criteria for picking a transcendent language. It comes from the word "Mag" which means "seed". Using my poetic license, I would say that Magyar is a "Star seed language", because of the obvious value system it contains. In Magyar, the word for wealth or value is "vagyon" (pronounced vadjyon), and it actually means "Beingness". This language has retained the golden ratio orientation. The value system that it is founded on is not one of fear-based survival and the loosening up of chains. For this reason, it is an accurate and befitting language to support my attempts to offer explanations on a topic that is beyond duality verbiage.

Mind

The mind is a self-evolving, self-limiting, self-regulating, self-dividing, self-proportioning and "self-angling" multi-dimensional interface. Once the "self-angling" ability has been activated, and the mind is inter-woven with the body's intelligence, it will have the possibility of self-awareness.

Negy

Négy (pronounced 'neidge') means "four". In the coded language of Magyar, which can be read backward and forward, "igen" read backward becomes "n**egy**" (the "Y" and the "I" in this context are interchangeable), which contains the "egy", which means Oneness. In these numbers - **egy** (1) and negy (4) - it clearly shows that we need to pay attention to the "four" since that's where the word "Igen" makes its return home through the elevation of the "**egy**" (one) to "n**egy**" (four) by adding the letter 'n.'

Portal

The "portal" is the point of entry, where the "angular" leap from the contrast-reality to the Ratio-reality takes place. There are 2 kinds of portals:

-The "***Life-Created Portal***" - the "portal" that we access when life gives us a shock and creates an interruption, such as losing our job, falling ill etc.

-The "***Self-Created Portal***" – the "portal" that we can create when life is good. This "portal" is created by using our "freed will" and by combining the "interruption" and the "bypassing" techniques that are taught in my seminars.

Roskad

Roskad (pronounded 'rosh-kad') literally means "to collapse under a heavy load". When decoded from presence, it indicates that something is collapsing under a heavy load, and because it is ancient (of the original ratio-based nature), it is collapsing under the golden ratio. In other words, "I am naturally collapsing... surrendering... converging or merging back into the ancient body (recognized as the ratio- based body) of God... not in a linear mode, but in the coded way that is in keeping with the golden ratio." While ***Rostokol*** is the action, the doing/non-doing, the ***Roskad***, is what happens as a result of the surrendered action of the ***Rostokol***.

Rostokol

The Magyar word Rostokol (pronounced 'rosh-tok-ol') is understood as "I'm sort of hanging out". In decoding this word from presence, it denotes "ancient body-ing" - as if the body itself were a verb. The "ancient body" refers to the original creation, when it was known and experienced that the body of man was a replica of the universe, since it was made in the image and likeness of the same ratio (the golden ratio) that the creator used to create everything. In other words, "the action to take in the direction of the 'ancient body'... without any expectation". So, the translation would be "I'm just sort of sitting... BEING here...being IN the original body... without any anticipation or expectation."

Self-Angling

Self-angling is the inner focused attention that leads to the "angular leap" by creating an internal vortex, in order to converge with the unifying forces of golden ratio reality.

Sirens

The Sirens were beautiful but dangerous creatures, according to Greek mythology, that lured the sailors with their beautiful voices to their doom, causing the ships to crash on the reefs near their island. A well-known encounter is described in the Odyssey. Odysseus plugged the crew's ears with wax and ordered them to bind him on the mast of the ship. He also told them that no matter how much he begged, they should not untie him. When they passed near the Sirens' island, Odysseus started begging his shipmates to let him go, but none heard him; instead, they tied him even more.

In the spiritual world, the Sirens are forever lurking at the "Aha Gates", waiting to ambush us and sabotage our possibility of awakening, by pretending to offer improvements to our existing contrast-reality.

The Sirens are those points along the way where we get lured and conned by paths, teachings or practices that are outer, shinier, more mysterious, more spiritual-sounding, more intellectual, more reputable, more fashionable, more dogmatic etc. - all of which act as Sirens who call us sweetly and pull us and our attention to their dangerous domain – the intellectual "Aha Gates" type of modalities. They ensure that we never really turn within. They all sound so good and so spiritual, as they fill our heads with partial truths.

Smart Wheel

A "smart wheel" is what I call the conglomerate of inter-related mental activities, such as gathering, analysing, comparing and assessing information, creating mental templates, value systems and identities etc. These exist on each level of the "Aha Gates" steps. The interactive activities in each "smart wheel" operate in a way which is very beneficial in our day to day living, as they give us the ability to accumulate information and arrive at more and more advanced conclusions, realizations and understandings.

Sword of Presence

The "Sword of Presence" is an ability that the human mind possesses, but it has yet to be re-activated. This is the process by which we enter into the ratio-based reality from the normal contrast-based reality. Operating from this new (new to us... but has been there all along) platform, is what we call the "Sword of Presence". At the same moment when our body is activated, which we call the "Sword of Presence", we are already using that "Sword of Presence".

Vagyon

Vagyon (pronounced vadjyon) means wealth or value. In the ancient Magyar language, it also means "Beingness". This word points to the fact that the value system of Magyar is based on Beingness. It is not founded on fear-based survival, but rather on the wealth of the golden ratio.

ABOUT THE AUTHOR

Gabor is a spirited coach who frees people from thought addiction, allowing consciousness to awaken and to become the real guide.

Gabor nearly lost his life escaping from communist Hungary at the age of 18. He arrived in Canada with a single minded and insatiable thirst for his first love – power and material wealth. At the age of 30 he was already a multi-millionaire, had his black belt in Hap-Kido, and had degrees in business and engineering. However, he was not at all happy.

And so Gabor turned to his 2nd love – spirituality. He resided with and was initiated by a Shaman in Ecuador and lived in a forest in the U.S., attending Ramtha's School of Enlightenment. He also studied with teachers such as Burt Harding and Bob Proctor, and took every new age seminar within shooting distance. All these served as soul searching pacifiers with an occasional glimmer of "What a great experience! If only I could hang on to it a bit longer."

Finally, at the age of 40, Gabor found his true Master – suffering. His suffering came in the forms of heartbreak, the loss of his family and his entire fortune, and suicidal depression. Through the grace of this newfound master, Gabor was now able to surrender to his 3rd and ultimate love – Presence, the silence of nothing, where the capitulated mind takes a back seat and becomes the servant.

Having deepened his presence and integrating it into his life, Gabor developed many techniques and the ability to teach the indescribable. For the past 10 years, he has been offering seminars and private sessions, online and in several countries around the globe. In these sessions, Gabor not only guides people and teaches the techniques he has developed, but he also helps them deal with the mind's onslaughts by proxy.

For more information, please visit: www.gaborharsanyi.com

ABOUT NURIT OREN

Nurit Oren, CPCC, is a Canadian Certified Professional Co-Active Coach, a Certified Witz Management/ Leadership Trainer and a Certified Art of Transformation Guide. Over the past 20 years, Nurit has helped countless individuals from all walks of life make life-changing decisions from the heart, by creating a safe space for inner wisdom and courage to guide them in the direction that is right for them, and free them from being stuck in unwanted situations.

Nurit is also a public speaker, an award-winning playwright and the author of "The Blind Leading the Blonde on the Road to Freedom: Confessions of a Recovering Spiritual Junkie". Her book is the story of her 40 years of intense spiritual seeking in several countries and with many teachers; the mistakes, the pitfalls and the elusive bliss along the way. It also describes how she finally found the truth after meeting Gabor (www.gaborharsanyi.com) who guided her into the "No-Thought Presence", upon which the realization dawned on her that all her previous pursuits were none other than a mind with an ego attempting to become enlightened.

Nurit now manages Gabor Harsanyi's activities and programs and she also interviews awakened beings and spiritual leaders from all over the world. Her interviews can be found on the "Conversations with Nurit" page on her website: www.nuritoren.com.

CPSIA information can be obtained
at www.ICGtesting.com
Printed in the USA
LVHW081757100319
609391LV00037B/472/P

9 789631 286076